EPowerment

Achieving Empowerment in the E World

DR. IZZY JUSTICE

iUniverse, Inc.
New York Bloomington

EPowerment
Achieving Empowerment in the E World

iUniverse books may be ordered through booksellers or by contacting:

iUniverse
1663 Liberty Drive
Bloomington, IN 47403
www.iuniverse.com
1-800-Authors (1-800-288-4677)

Because of the dynamic nature of the Internet, any Web addresses or links contained in this book may have changed since publication and may no longer be valid. The views expressed in this work are solely those of the author and do not necessarily reflect the views of the publisher, and the publisher hereby disclaims any responsibility for them.

ISBN: 978-1-4502-2509-0 (sc)
ISBN: 978-1-4502-2511-3 (dj)
ISBN: 978-1-4502-2510-6 (ebook)

Printed in the United States of America

iUniverse rev. date: 04/23/2010

For Stephanie, Lexi, Hunter, and my eternal mentor,
Gary Mason

Contents

Foreword
by Marshall Goldsmith

We have the opportunity to learn today in ways that ten or twenty years ago we could not even have imagined. Technological breakthroughs, such as instant download, wireless networks, and audio-video transmission, are now commonly available around the world, connecting us in what has been called the global mind.

If everything is working properly, we are able to learn what we need to know, when we need to know it, and from the best source available to teach it. In fact, we are empowered. Unfortunately, as there is an increase in the amount of information in the global mind, it becomes more and more difficult to access meaningful information. Thus we drown in a sea of information, unable to access relevant information, searching for the tools that will help us to live and perform better—the tools that will empower us at the individual and organizational levels.

Dr. Izzy Justice makes a bold statement in EPowerment that such empowerment is finally achievable in the twenty-first century. To that end, he offers a new term: EPowerment—a fascinating concept that marries high emotional intelligence (EQ) and the collective human knowledge of the e world. And with examples, observations, and wisdom from professionals around the world, he guides us, in this exciting and forward-thinking book, to overhaul our way of thinking about work, the workplace, and knowledge, so that we might really achieve "empowerment." You must read this book if you and your workforce want to be competitive by appreciating the transformative times we live in. The confluence of previously disparate ideas here creates the perfect framework to empower ourselves.

Acknowledgments

Crafting this book was a true collaboration that I thoroughly enjoyed. The spirit of curiosity and exploration among over fifty highly credentialed industry practitioners, thought leaders, academics, entrepreneurs, and consultants is what led to this *magnum opus*.

I must start with Eva Rykr, who deserves tremendous credit for her research, coordination, ingenuity, and hard work. This book would not be possible without her.

I also need to thank Todd Harrison, Ruth Kennedy, Jane Luciano, Kelli Price, Susan Richter, and Linda Worden. I am deeply indebted to them for allowing me to conduct case studies in their organizations, their feedback on the content, and their incomparable spirit of true collaboration.

Also deserving great credit are Ana Dutra, Michelle Marquard, and Bob Wall for their rigorous review of the manuscript, editing, and constructive feedback. The final version would not be what it is without their input.

In addition, I want to thank the following folks for allowing me to tap into their unique perspectives on human capital matters—

Anne Feller, Troy Heflin, Effenus Henderson, Kevin Henry, Bill Hodgetts, Hy Pomerance, Tom Trainer, Karie Willyerd, and Bob Zierk.

Finally, many sincere thanks to all the inspiring leaders in the human capital field featured in chapter 10. Your unique perspectives provided the perfect closure to the book.

Introduction

When I left Africa to come to the United States for college in the eighties, I left a world that was several decades behind in so many ways. I remember my family getting a thirteen-inch color TV when I was a teenager, and I thought that man had conquered it all. To see the world in color was one of the more exciting childhood experiences I can recall, primarily because it stimulated a powerful imagination of possibilities. I desperately wanted to be a part of exploring those possibilities. Once in the States, I saw for the first time a CD player, a microwave, a computer, and a television with multiple channels. Whoa!

Little did I know just how much change our lives would continue to go through. At a seminar I facilitated recently, I asked the audience to list all the inventions of the past twenty-five years that are presently shaping the way we live and work. And then to juxtapose them with how we lived and worked the previous twenty-five years. It is no stretch to assert that the present generations have the highest probability of achieving their full potential in a way that no other set of human beings who have walked the face of this earth have. Just take a moment and think about this. If you want to be the best at what you do, can you honestly say "I can't find information on how to do it?"

To drive this point further, think of what the generations of the past could have done with all of our tools—all the available apps, blogs, BlackBerrys, cell phones, DVRs, Google, GPS, Facebook, iPods, Skype, Netflix, texting (just think, *110 billion* text messages were sent in December 2008), Wikipedia, Twitter, and YouTube, to name just a few of the knowledge and information exchange inventions of the past decade alone.

Human knowledge—past, present, and future—is widely accessible in unprecedented ways. The power of constant connection should never again be underestimated or underutilized. We were never able to constantly connect until we possessed cell phones and other mobile devices, which are, of course, constantly on. New technological innovations of this decade will allow laptops to be constantly connected wirelessly instead of having to search for a connection. The imperative to leverage all this to perform at our best, to constantly enhance our self equity, and to live happier and healthier lives has never been greater and our chance of achieving it has also never been better.

I have spent all my adult life not in the imagination of possibilities but in the reality of them. As a management consultant with two global firms, I consulted with leaders and managers at organizations all over the world. I became fascinated by the term empowerment. I loved it like most people did and felt we've been getting closer and closer to it since the '80s. Driven in large part by technology, as more and more knowledge and tools became available to us, both in our personal and professional lives, we did indeed become more efficient, but not necessarily empowered. Something was still missing.

It was about fifteen years ago that I was first exposed to

emotional intelligence. Eureka! I finally had a framework around what I had always known—our ever-changing emotions play a significant role in our performance. Our ability to recognize and alter them based on the demands of the situation is the missing link.

This book, a powerful collaboration of thought leaders, practitioners, and academics, marinated with a blend of rigorous research and real-world applications of forward-thinking ideas, is a culmination of that journey I began as an immigrant teenager from Africa toward the ultimate state of personal and professional empowerment. I still wake up and view this country and the world as a land and life of constant opportunity. I read a philosophical quote that said, "Doubt the man who has found the truth, but trust the man who is searching for it." It is incredible to live in times where it is not the "knowers" but the "learners" who will thrive.

I am thrilled to share with you a powerful new concept—EPowerment: an amalgam of achieving empowerment in the e world we now live in and leveraging your own inherent emotional intelligence. I am convinced that the content of this book will help you think about just how achievable empowerment is for you and your organization. As you read this book, ask yourself, "Can I afford not to be empowered?"

—Dr. Izzy Justice

Chapter 1
Why EPowerment and Why Now?

Sixty percent of U.S. organizations report that they plan to focus more on high-potential employees.[1]

Empowerment means allowing people at appropriate levels of an organization to know that they are capable of, *and* accountable for, making business decisions without having to fight through layers of bureaucracy and inefficient business processes, both formal and informal ones. Who does not want to feel empowered? What could possibly be wrong with this concept?

When the term *empowerment* found its way to the workplace, it generated a lot of excitement. The expectation was that adults would be treated as adults, high expectations would be set and achieved, and decision-making and innovation would be accelerated. But putting it into practice proved to be easier said than done, and the excitement soon fizzled out.[2] Why do we fail to achieve empowerment?

The problem isn't with the concept itself or even with support for the concept. There are two fundamental reasons why

1

empowerment hasn't been successful in the past twenty years in our organizations.

First, the information necessary to make decisions never quite finds its way to those front-line managers, leaders, and employees supposedly empowered to make decisions. Either the data is not accessible in real time or it becomes diluted as it trickles its way down from upper management, rendering the information less useful. In some cases, the data is even outdated, causing the decision maker to either make the wrong decision or defer the decision entirely.

The second reason is that without proper training and the right information at the right time, the front-line employees find it too risky to make decisions and throw them back upward. They have not had the opportunity to learn to be resourceful. Both the organizational culture and the level of individual courage fail to support empowerment. Organizational rewards and incentive programs have historically not been aligned with empowerment either. Why risk the visibility of poor decisions and adversely impact one's career? This risk-taking fortitude, or lack thereof, is the core component of Emotional Intelligence, introduced in chapter 3.

As a result of these two factors, empowerment failed to live up to its promise. Companies continued to struggle with poor decisions, too much micromanagement, workplace dissatisfaction, and the "it's not *my* problem" syndrome. Empowerment was not organically supported in the ecosystem of the organization, nor were the inhabitants ready for it.

> *"Many companies are attracted by a fantasy version*
> *of empowerment and simultaneously repelled by*
> *the reality. How lovely to have energetic, dedicated*

workers who always seize the initiative (but only when "appropriate"), who enjoy taking risks (but never risky ones), who volunteer their ideas (but only brilliant ones), who solve problems on their own (but make no mistakes), who aren't afraid to speak their minds (but never ruffle any feathers), who always give their very best to the company (but ask no unpleasant questions about what the company is giving them back). How nice it would be, in short, to empower workers without giving them any power."[3]

But we are in the second decade of the new millennium now. Organizations have undergone significant changes that bode well for empowerment. The workforce itself has also changed in ways that create a readiness for empowerment. What if empowerment was ready for a comeback? What if now is not only the best time to realize it, but also the most necessary time to realize it? When it was first introduced, perhaps it was just another nice business management concept. Today, empowerment is a business imperative. *Harnessing the individual and collective potential of employees is the singular imperative of this decade.*

In this book, we will present some very compelling arguments as to why empowerment is finally achievable. *More importantly, we will argue why empowerment in 2010 and beyond should be the number one priority of all organizations. We will also discuss how to achieve this empowerment state at both the individual and organization levels.*

We will introduce a new term—**EPowerment**—an amalgam of **E**mpowerment, high **E**motional intelligence (EQ), and harnessing the power of the e world (**E**lectronically-enabled accessibility to knowledge, irrespective of where it exists, whether organically in a person, a community, or inorganically in easily accessible sources of knowledge). Collective human knowledge, which allows all of us to live and perform better, is becoming easier to access and will very quickly become freely available.

EPowerment involves:

1. *Eliminating* barriers to the access of knowledge and information.

2. Creating a fearless, *emotionally intelligent* workforce that is willing to expand its own potential.

3. Building a culture that practices, nourishes, and rewards employee *engagement*.

4. Developing business practices that are *environmentally* responsible and in tune with an age that is coming to terms with global learning.

But why now? Why is now the time for EPowerment?

We will share several reasons, but it is worth noting that, based on the collective set of changes and trends, empowerment has never been more achievable and more necessary than now.

The Changing Face of the Workplace
That Was Then

The generations following World War II carved out what was then a new workplace. People went to work and stayed with the same company for years. The cubicle world was born, sometimes resulting in huge rooms filled with faceless workers hunched over typewriters that were eventually replaced by computer screens.

Organizations were marked by rigid hierarchical structures. Careers were considered in terms of climbing the ladder. We measured success by attaining ever-more-impressive titles, expanding our number of direct reports, and, if we were blessed, by finally establishing a foothold in the corner office. Job satisfaction was less important than stability, investing for retirement, and making sure that we never lost our place in line. Staying visible became so important that many people would work for years without even taking a vacation.

Today, things have changed dramatically. The modern employer expects the employee to work within more abstract, undefined parameters, and the employee expects to have all the tools necessary to make better decisions. Waiting for this to occur is no longer feasible: both sides want EPowerment *now*.

Fifty-six percent of employers in the United States are experiencing a leadership shortage that is impeding their organization's performance.[4] This is not a secret. Fifty-two percent of employees said there were not enough qualified managers in their organizations today and 78 percent reported either that they aren't sure that their companies have enough qualified people to fill future leadership jobs or that they firmly believe that they do not (45 percent of those were of the firm opinion that businesses were going to face a shortage of qualified managers in the future[5]).

If you look at the world today and the world twenty-five to thirty years ago, the rate of change has increased. It's not that things were never changing. The rules were set and established, and if you wanted to be successful in your career or in business, you learned the rules, got good at them, and that was it. That being said, there is a basic set of leadership competencies that continue to be useful and important. They haven't gone away. However, one of the biggest changes is that for many reasons, such as the development of new technologies and the growth of the global economy, the rate of change has continued to accelerate. A world has been created in which the rules are constantly changing. Leaders need to deal with complexity, ambiguity, and rules that aren't clear. The winners will be those who create new rules. There have always been entrepreneurs at the birth of some new technology, but the speed at which this is happening and the constancy of it is astounding. The old model was innovation–plateau–stability–innovation, but now we are in a period where the change is constant and exponential. Our new world requires a whole new level of thinking and operating on the part of leaders in order to thrive in an environment like that.

—Bill Hodgetts, VP of corporate leadership
development, Fidelity

It is predicted that, moving forward, the average tenure of an employee in an organization will be around five years—this is a *rent* model. Both employees and employers are essentially renting each other. This is quite different from the *ownership* model of the past. We all know just how different it feels when you rent something versus owning it. The sense of commitment and ethic is different. Leaders will have to figure out how to create an *ownership* culture in a renter's world to maximize performance, innovation, and collaboration. They will have to create an empowerment culture. Jane Luciano, VP of global learning and organization development at Bristol-Myers Squibb says to her employees, "While I cannot promise employment, I can promise you employability—you will learn and acquire new skills here that will further your career."

Globalization

Traditionally, the term "globalization," from a business perspective, has meant that multinational companies have offices and employees all over the world. The meaning of the term then transitioned to incorporate outsourcing. Outsourcing meant that jobs were transferred from domestic locations in the West to other parts of the world because employing workers in other locations was, in most cases, cheaper, faster, and, in some cases, actually better.

Now, globalization is an important issue in a much different context from that of the past fifteen years. Today, globalization must incorporate yet another dimension. It is the idea that we can now instantly connect with more people in more parts of the world with more frequency and in a geographically boundless manner. In many cases, it is not unusual to communicate and collaborate with co-workers, suppliers, vendors, and customers from all over the world on a daily basis in much the same way we historically did when working with fellow employees on a different floor of the same building. And because the playing field (in the context of skills and performance) is somewhat leveled now, there is a tremendous amount of reliance on the ability to work effectively with this tremendously diverse workforce, whose members are all competing for similar goals. So globalization brings diversity. The companies that are going to be most successful will be those whose leaders and teams are best able to work with people from a broad variety of cultures and countries-of-origin in a mobile workforce.

In this century of a global workforce where we interact with not just more people, but more people with diverse backgrounds, our ability to navigate through the complexity of human behavior is paramount. Ruth Kennedy, director of organization development at VF Corporation says, "Leaders will have to have a way to deal with an increasingly global focus. That requires a lot of going with the flow. They must have a foundation to deal with that."

That foundation is our emotions. Embedded in all forms of diversity is the one thing we all have in common—emotions. All humans have the same basic set of emotions that govern thought and behavior. Leaders who understand how to deal with emotion and focus people on a shared strategy will be best able to engage and lead in this flatter global workforce. This will be discussed at length in chapter 3.

Implications of Generational Differences

Any discussion of the nature of work must factor generational changes into the equation. Baby boomers will exert one of the largest demographic influences on the nature of work. This is partly due to their numbers, given that they make up more than 38 percent of the workforce.[6] More importantly, they aren't going anywhere, at least not yet.

The 2008–2009 recession saw huge losses in investment portfolios and retirement accounts worldwide. During that time, major U.S. equity indexes were sharply negative, with the S&P 500 Index losing 37 percent for 2008.[7] As a result, only 13 percent of workers say they are very confident about having enough money for a comfortable retirement, the lowest percentage ever recorded.[8] Consequently, huge numbers of people who had planned to retire earlier are now holding on to their jobs for far longer than they had planned. Investment firm T. Rowe Price calculates that the oldest boomers will have to delay retirement by nearly nine years in order to recover what they lost in the market[9]. Research by the Employee Benefits Institute found that just 23 percent of boomers age fifty-five and older have more than $250,000 in savings and investments.[10]

Retirement used to come in steady waves, allowing for smooth transitions as sixty-somethings left the workforce, making room for younger workers. This time, though, the unemployment rate hovered near, and in some states, surpassed 10 percent for the first time in decades[11] — in part because the normal retirement cycle had been disrupted.

Boomers are holding on to their jobs en masse, blocking younger workers from advancing in the workplace. According to the Center for Labor Market Studies at Northeastern University, employment rates for teens and twenty-somethings this past decade have fallen, while the number of Americans aged 55 and older who have jobs has gone up.[12] Just 20 percent of 2009 college graduates who applied for a job during the recession actually found one.[13]

The "War for Talent," discussed heavily prior to the recession, has lost much attention. But studies continue to show that delayed retirement is just that—a delay. There still will be more than seventy million baby boomers who *want* to leave the workplace and go do something more meaningful with their lives, which in many cases means getting away from corporate America and all the emotional stress that has piled up from that world. These baby boomers still want to be active and even work, but they want to do so under their terms. Flexibility is the key here: 87 percent of boomers say that having flexible work options is important; 83 percent of boomers say that work/life balance matters to them; and two thirds want to work remotely.[14] The boomers' departure from the workplace will have a significant impact on businesses everywhere. Their presence will be missed, creating a void of knowledge, experience, and wisdom. The change will be deeply profound and impact empowerment at both the individual and organization levels. What substitute is there for the hands-on experience and meaningful relationships that take years to cultivate?

By 2019, Generation X (born between 1965 and 1978) will have spent nearly two decades in the workplace. They will be leading a workforce that will have transformed almost beyond recognition. There will be more younger employees in management and leadership roles than ever before. Younger leaders will be occupying roles with an average of nine years less experience than the previous generation.[15] A thirty-year-old must be able to not just tactically perform as a forty-year-old, but to also make sound decisions with the maturity of a forty-year-old. These less experienced professionals will need to find ways to develop this kind of wisdom quickly. Those individuals and organizations that do so will have an upper hand.

Generation Y (born between 1979 and 2000) are just as numerous as the boomers, but that will not prevent the imminent dilemma. Generation Y realizes it is now pointless to put in long years of effort at any one company in exchange for a series of raises and promotions. "Paying your dues, moving up slowly, and getting the corner office—that's going away. In ten years, it will be gone," says Bruce Tulgan, head of the New Haven, Conn. consulting firm Rainmaker Thinking and author of *Not Everyone Gets a Trophy*. It will be less common to discuss success in terms of rank, seniority, or power. Instead, success can be anything that matters to you personally. Moreover, companies are changing as well, making room for more short-term independent contractors, freelancers, and consultants—and fewer traditional employees.

Empowerment for the younger generation is no longer a perk or luxury, it is an expectation. Make no mistake—the best workers will gravitate, consciously or subconsciously, to people and organizations that meet this expectation. This is already happening and is in part what has led to a burst of social entrepreneurship within generation Y. Steve Fritz, president of VF Outlet, part of VF Corporation, recommends, "You need to hear Generation Y out and give them a platform to present ideas." The younger generations are actually smarter and infinitely more resourceful.

The Flynn Effect describes the rise in IQ test scores over generations, across time. This is a worldwide effect representing changes in not only intelligence, but also in certain types of memory. Over the past sixty years, IQ scores have risen by twenty points. This means that a child of average intelligence back in the 1930s would be classified as mildly retarded today.[16] The leading explanation is that environmental changes arose from effects of modernization, things like intellectually demanding work, more use of technology, and more attention paid to children. This means that people get more practice at manipulating abstract concepts. We are evolving to adapt to complexity!

Gen Y may not know how valuable they are today. However, it is precisely due to their higher EQ that they will figure out their value much more quickly than the other generations will and may outpace the Gen Xers for key roles in businesses if the Gen Xers do not adapt quickly.

—Todd Harrison, director of leadership and associate development, WelPoint

The Future of Work
Susan Richter, Food Lion, LLC

If you look at the future of work, people are asking for something very different from what we are accustomed to. The way we work, how we work, and the jobs we do are all changing. Recently, we honored associates who have worked here for thirty years, and I don't see that happening in the future. Careers will still be thirty years, but not at the same company. Employees will, primarily, use the knowledge they gain to better their careers, even if it means leaving the company that has taught them this. So now the question is, "How do we harness this investment? How do we motivate people to stay—without imposing binding contracts? If we know we will only keep them for three to five years, how do we use that to our advantage—in selection, retention, and empowerment?"

Given the workforce of the future, the way we develop people will be different than it has been in the past. In the past, high performance was all about metrics, and we rewarded people who were able to execute—those who got the most sales and achieved profitability got the rewards. There was nothing there about developing people, and we didn't give much thought to the collaboration involved in that effort. Now we are working with fifty years of history and focusing on leadership development. The vision is to have trusted, caring connections that energize everyone—today, tomorrow, together. The goal is to create a culture of high performance. We are raising the bar and bringing out the best in every associate and not accepting mediocrity. Success will now be measured by questions such as, "How do I engage the associates on my team, have I set the context, do they understand why we are doing this? Do employees see the connection between satisfied customers, higher profits, and their work environment? Do they see the big picture?" To cope with the new world, we are at a pivot point where we are completely changing the way we are doing things and how we are recognizing and rewarding people.

The Emergence of Women in Leadership

The presence of women is one of the forces changing the nature of work as women come to play increasingly important roles in leadership. Their more relationship-oriented leadership is perfect for nurturing the collaboration of knowledge workers and creating a culture of empowerment. Women are consensus builders, conciliators, and collaborators, and they employ what is called a transformational leadership style—heavily engaged, motivational, and extremely well suited for the emerging, less hierarchical workplace.

Within just ten years, we'll see a more fluid and more virtual workforce that demands the type of management skills that women tend to possess. Women will move rapidly up the chain of command to where emotional intelligence skills will become even more beneficial.[17]

Women manage more cautiously than men do.[18] They focus on the long term, while men thrive on risk, especially when they are surrounded by other men. How different will our workforce be when leadership has a more strategic perspective and a more inclusive style, and uses it to communicate transparently with an empowered workforce?

> *I am a work in progress. I am a leader, but my leadership philosophy is to lead from behind. As part of this servant leadership mentality, I use a lot of different tools and techniques that I'll never get credit for. I lead fifty clients. If my clients are successful thanks to my help, then I have been a success. I am not there for the glory, I am there for them.*
>
> –Anne Feller, Cox Communications

In today's marketplace, the female leadership style is not only distinctly different but also essential. Women's long-term focus is already having an impact on organizational results. The workplace-research group Catalyst studied 353 Fortune 500 companies and found that those with the most women in senior management positions had a higher return on equities—by more than a third.[19] The empowerment model embedded in the natural female style is clearly a major success factor.

> *One of the greatest lessons in leadership I have ever learned is that leadership is not about me, but rather about those that I serve. To become a truly great leader, we have to put others before ourselves. If we don't, we may lead for a little while, but ultimately we'll turn around and find that no one is following us anymore.*
>
> —Caz Matthews, president of the WellPoint Foundation

Changes in Corporate Culture

Knowledge workers thrive on collaboration and participation in decision-making. The last years have seen many experiments in organizational structure and functioning to encourage collaboration, and ultimately, empowerment.

> *I send a message to employees that they are important, that I care about them, and that I trust them. To achieve that, I empower them accordingly. I push decisions down as much as possible.*
>
> —Bob Zierk, VP of human resources, Black & Decker

When a company gives employees freedom, productivity goes up. Capital One does not mandate office time from their knowledge workers and neither does Best Buy.[20] Best Buy's corporate office implemented a system called ROWE—results-only work environment—and found that productivity skyrocketed by 40 percent. Similarly, Gap also piloted ROWE[21] and found productivity increased 21 percent, quality improved 15 percent, engagement scores spiked from 67 percent to 86 percent, and work/life balance scores rose from 72 percent to 82 percent. In a results-only work environment, the metrics of performance are not the inputs, but the outputs. This means that employees can work whenever, wherever they choose, as long as deadlines are met and outcomes are achieved. Organizations will no longer have an incentive to fill buildings with cubicles of workers who do lots of work without much result. Flexibility is no longer a benefit; it's a compelling business strategy. But thriving in a flexible environment will not come easily or without adaptation.

Leaders of organizations will increasingly face the demand to create open, collaborative environments. Those who grew up in a top-down, hierarchical style of leadership will find that they can no longer just tell people what to do and expect them to do it. Knowledge workers need a deep understanding of corporate goals and strategy, and they thrive in conditions that allow them to exert their influence on corporate thinking.

> *I have grown into my current leadership philosophy, and if I were to comment on this ten years ago, you would be reading a very different answer. I view leadership as a privilege as opposed to a right. It is a privilege that is earned. It is gifted by those you are given the honor and accountability to lead. The*

notion is that other people (those you are leading) give you the authority to lead them. They give it to you willingly and generously, as opposed to you mandating their followership through your authority because you have been named a leader by the title on your business card.

—Kevin Henry, chief HR officer, Coca-Cola
Bottling Consolidated Co.

People engaged in leadership development and talent management are already looking for ways to identify and develop the leadership skills necessary to nurture collaboration. Tomorrow's leadership development must feature more effective strategies than today's event-based training schedules. The personal changes necessary for developing a collaborative leadership culture mandate a fundamental shift in how we select and train leaders in the future. The traditional workshop approach to development may be enough to impart information, but it does not begin to produce the personal insights and profound change necessary to manage or lead in a collaborative environment.

There are several universal and enduring traits that contribute to effective leadership. Effective leadership is comprised of technical competence, communication, interpersonal skills, and technological savvy. There is a growing interest in transparency and sustainability. Social networks will reshape business and how we connect.

—Effenus Henderson, chief diversity officer,
Weyerhaeuser

Changes in the Nature of Work

To visualize the workplace of the next few years, first consider what work is going to be like. The capability to connect to both people and information by technology from anywhere and at anytime will transform the way we work.

If there was any benefit to the recession, it was the reality check it provided. We discovered that if we focus on *what* must get done rather than *where* or *how* it gets done, more will get done. The traditional way is coming to an end. We are at an inflection point. The sooner that this is discovered and integrated with how things were done before, the more opportunity for success there is.

Such a change in work can only be driven by the collaborative technologies enabling living and thriving in the e world. Having the tools is necessary but not sufficient. An ability to create the necessary personal and communal comfort and trust will be just as relevant.

A New Approach to Leadership

Agility/Adaptive Leadership—Do not get attached to the way things are. Guaranteed, they will be different tomorrow. The world is not static, and thus requires continuous adaptation to different people, experiences, and circumstances. Adaptive leadership allows for adjusting to such factors while still maintaining a focus on the core values and strategies. Such leadership requires the ability to empathize with others with whom you share a vision. When a leader can manage the needs of multiple stakeholders in complex situations is when a leader can make a true difference in today's world. But the knowledge to do so does not and will not come from a book or a seminar. It takes years of self-learning, supplemented by outside wisdom.

The release of traditional methods will mean an increasing emphasis on hiring people on a project basis. The management, scientific, and technical consulting services industries (all industries with a high percentage of contract work) are projected to increase by 82.8 percent between 2008 and 2018.[22] Jobs of the future will have very little to do with processing words or numbers or running errands. Instead, the focus will be on essential, high-potential people solving strategic problems and doing collaborative work. The remainder of the work will be outsourced and contracted. These are two very different skill sets, by the way. The areas of talent management and workforce planning require a new set of skills for human resource practitioners as well.

Conservative, moderate, and aggressive estimates of the number of U.S. jobs that could potentially be moved offshore in the coming decades are roughly 22 percent, 26 percent, and 29 percent, respectively, according to Jagdish Bhagwati and Alan S. Blinder, authors of *Offshoring of American Jobs.* That corresponds to thirty million to forty million jobs.[23]

Largest employment declines from 2006 to 2016

Occupation	Decrease in Demand
Stock clerks and order fillers	-131,000
Cashiers, except gaming	-118,000
Packers and packagers, hand	-104,000
File clerks	-97,000
Order clerks	-66,000
Telemarketers	-39,000
Inspectors, testers, sorters, samplers, weighers	-35,000
Computer operators	-32,000
Driver/sales workers	-24,000
Word processors and typists	-21,000
Switchboard Operators	-15,000
Data entry keyers	-15,000

The most desired jobs will be those that include interaction with people—managing customers, organizing fans, engaging others in social media. The need for designers and creativity will not go away. We will still need to brainstorm.

But this work can be done virtually. It is too expensive, too slow, and plainly, too inefficient, for a couple of hundred people to congregate at one central physical location. Instead of aggregating people and sharing tactical information, we will move toward capturing meaningful knowledge and sharing human connections.

Consider that it takes an average of twenty-four minutes to refocus our attention after an interruption. And interruptions eat up 28 percent of the work day.[24] In a virtual setting, we can sign off or put up an "away" message in order to focus on priorities— conserving precious emotional energy.

The e world makes working as a team, synchronized to a shared goal, easier and more productive than ever. But, as in a three-legged-race, you'll instantly know when a teammate is struggling because that will slow you down as well. Many people will embrace this new high-stress, high-speed, high-flexibility way of work. They'll go from a few days alone at home, maintaining the status quo, to urgent team sessions, sometimes in person but often online. It will make still other people yearn for jobs like those in the old days, when we fought traffic, sat in a cube, typed memos, took a long lunch, and then sat in traffic again.

> *There will be an evolution of skill sets. Knowledge is doubling, yet it takes ten years to become an expert. People will rely less and less on knowledge in their heads and instead on skills to find the knowledge. We'll be integrators—ability to analyze, think, research, collaborate (EQ is a huge component of*

*one's ability to collaborate). People who have the
skill set to keep up with the advances in technologies
will experience success.*

—Karie Willyerd, CLO, Sun Microsystems

Recession Recovery: The Future is Already Here

As a result of the 2008–2009 economic recession, companies in all industries and across various geographic regions have been seeking to do more with less. Leaders are hunting with a vengeance to find cheaper and better ways to do more than they were doing before.

*It has become more and more apparent, thanks to
the crisis that self-awareness, inclusion/diversity,
self-management, and holistic/systems thinking will
be the key skills to success.*

—Troy Heflin, VP of organizational
development, Volvo

There was something alarmingly different about this recession than the previous three economic slowdowns of the past twenty-five years. When budgets are tight and layoffs mandated with grim frequency, people naturally think about how to cut back. But this time around, the malaise has been so communal, so prevalent, and so very personal (whose retirement fund did not shrink by half?) that these themes have developed new meaning. We all started saving instead of spending. This time, the need to do more with less was more than wishful thinking—it has become our new reality.

The recession hit everyone so hard that it is making most

people say, "let's not put ourselves in this situation again." Rather than just waiting for a recession to end so that we can get back to normal, businesses are establishing a new normal. And whether they realize it or not, they are embracing EPowerment.

Every expenditure and priority must now be examined with this "new normal" in mind. This has resulted in a paradigm shift in talent development. The days of sending managers and leaders off to exotic locations for week-long seminars or conferences are gone. Throwing in golf and spa amenities is being viewed as a career-ending move instead of an attendance-enhancing technique. Off-site learning and development will continue to exist but not in the manner to which we've been accustomed. Leaders in organizations want to see a tangible ROI—they want to see how that $7,500 trip resulted in something clearly beneficial for the individual or the corporation. They also want to be able to track it and explain it. What did people learn? How will they transfer their new knowledge to improve the organization? How will this training lead to EPowerment?

The economy that we experienced in late 2008 and all of 2009 has had a fundamental and paradigm-shifting impact on not just the working professional but also on the organization. Most of us have been hurt in some form or another. Whether it was watching our savings literally disappear, losing a job, being overworked, or reducing traditional spending and consumption, in some way, we've all been affected by this recession. The impact has not just been a financial or vocational one; it has been a profoundly emotional one. We can compare it to post-traumatic stress disorder (PTSD)—the emotional stress experienced by veterans of wars or survivors of other traumatic experiences. The trust in employers, in institutions, in government, in leaders, and in some basic truths about workplace behavior has eroded. Consider that just 36 percent of employees believe that top managers at their company act with honesty and integrity.[25] Survival mode behavior has indeed taken its toll. So, as we exit the recession, organizations and leaders have to be emotionally ready to deal with an apathetic and fatigued workforce. This is again why EQ is more relevant now than ever.

Talent management will continue to be a major human capital issue over the coming decade. Just prior to the recession, in 2007, the Department of Labor had predicted a shortage of about three million workers in 2012. Though delayed now, we anticipate that the shortage will still occur. As discussed, baby boomers will begin to make their anticipated exit. The knowledge economy will dominate the Western world as the globalization trend of outsourcing blue-collar needs continues.

These fundamental changes in the nature of work itself foretell radical changes in what we do and how we do it. But this book is not intended to be futuristic. Instead, this book explores *how* we will work, not *what* we will be doing in the not too distant future.

> *The ability to collaborate and authentically engage with others will be the key competency of the future. Bring your own potential but also be able to suspend it to allow others to collaborate. Adaptability and resilience are really important so you can learn and adapt as business needs you to.*
>
> —Kelli Price, senior vice president of people, Premier, Inc.

Nobody is immune from misreading the future. In 1899, Charles H. Durell of the U.S. Patent Office said that everything that was going to be invented had already been invented. In 1951, Cambridge mathematician Douglas Hartree said that the three computers then in existence did math so quickly that no more would ever need to be manufactured. "No one else will ever need machines of their own or be able to afford them." In 1968, the notable journal *BusinessWeek* went so far as to state, "With more than fifteen types of foreign cars already on sale here, the Japanese car industry isn't likely to carve out a big share of the market for itself." Even the notable business giant Bill Gates is reported to have once said that no one would ever need more than 640 kilobytes of memory. Soothsayers operate at their own risk.

Nevertheless, we'll examine how advances in technology, the availability of social networks, changes in demographics, and our refined understanding of human beings and work combine to foretell how we will work in the coming years. More importantly, you will learn what your business should already be doing today, as well as what you need to be doing to prepare for the future.

As you read, you will find it helpful to ask yourself the following questions:

- Is your business taking advantage of opportunities described in these pages?
- What do you need to be doing individually to make this happen?
- How do our findings affect your business today?
- What will happen to your company's competitiveness if you don't adequately take our findings into account in planning for the future?
- Are you EPowered? Are your employees? Is your organization?

In the next three chapters, and before we get to *how* to achieve EPowerment, we will dive more deeply into the three Es that comprise EPowerment: technology (e world), emotional intelligence (EQ), and empowerment. Having this context will allow you to fully understand just how powerful these components are for the next decade, and it will provide better meaning for the five principles we will present as critical to achieving EPowerment. These five principles can be used to transform yourself and your organizations (the "how to"), and should be considered foundational to every individual and organization that wants to not only survive but thrive in the coming years.

Summary and Key Points

- Empowerment failed to fully live up to its promise.
- Empowerment fizzled out due to lack of training, not enough management support, diluted messages from company leaders, insufficient access to up-to-date information, and the degree of risk involved in making decisions in an unsupportive environment.
- Organizations have undergone significant structural and cultural changes.
- EPowerment is empowerment enabled by technological connectivity and emotional intelligence.
- The global economy and a diverse workforce make EPowerment all the more relevant.
- Younger generations take to new technologies naturally and expect empowerment.
- Women are more prominent in the workplace, naturally leading with an empowerment style.
- The rise of knowledge workers makes empowerment essential.
- These changes make empowerment a business imperative.
- Harnessing the individual and collective potential of employees is the singular imperative for all organizations during this decade.

Chapter 2
The E World

The e world – a super connected world.

If, in the last ten years, our lives have undergone much change due to new technologies, I forecast that the upcoming decade will be one of sea change in our lives and workplaces.

We are using today's leading-edge technologies to design and build tomorrow's possibilities, which seem endless, but the application of the "not yet invented," further integrated into what we are still adapting to, will have profound effects on how we live and work.

This integration, allied to an ever-shrinking adoption timeframe within which we must absorb it, will continue to influence, dis-intermediate, and disrupt businesses and competition as well as our lives, and not always for the better.

We will see an increase in the speed of change of new, agile business models and the resulting impact on business processes, organizational structures, jobs, roles, tools, training and education, and mentoring needs. We will also be seeing the physical workplace morph ever faster into a virtual workplace where at least some of the work can be done by employees in their homes, at "the office" if it still exists as such, and at the outsourcer in the United States and abroad, with more companies evolving their information-based products and services to a twenty-four-hours-per–day, seven-days–a-week, "follow the sun" manufacturing model with virtual teams around the country and the world working essentially in the same business process and with the outcomes passed on to the next "shift" as though in a 24x7 factory. This model has certainly been in place for more than ten years—I utilized it in the late '90s, and, as it is further enabled with more bandwidth and the capabilities of "The Cloud," (the concept has been around since the '70s by the way), it promises to provide compelling value propositions for profit-hungry business.

So, just as the traveler can now check in from home, pro athletes have joined the ranks of paid "Twitterers," social networking has been revolutionized via Facebook and the iPhone, DNA has revolutionized law enforcement and pharmaceutical drug developments, and we see ever-more computerized military arsenals, what can we expect to see just around the corner?

Lots of initiatives are under way, via social enterprises, to deliver improved quality of life, employment, and income to the so-called "Bottom of the Pyramid" poor countries of the world, which contain more people than the developed world and whose residents will have more access to clean water, electricity via totally new battery technology, Internet access, and health care delivered in some cases via "virtual surgery" as in today's battlefields. We will see totally new business models in the media industry where, for example, YouTube is fast overtaking TV as the most important entertainment medium, and vastly improved means of security, both cyber and physical, particularly as it relates to traveler safety.

Revolutionary business models like that of ZARA, a Spanish company quickly impacting the fashion industry, will provide unheard-of choice for the consumer as well as within the industry. ZARA has a super-responsive supply chain which allows them to continually design, produce, and deliver new garments into fifteen hundred stores in seventy-one countries worldwide in fifteen days, versus the contemporary model of having only a few seasons for introducing new products.

Clearly the possibilities, positive and negative, are amazing to comprehend.

—Tom Trainer, recipient of the Albert Einstein
Award for Information Technology and former
CIO at Reebok, PepsiCo, CitiGroup, and Eli Lilly

It is easy to forget that most of what is in this chapter has evolved in our lifetime, and, in fact, just in the last twenty-five years or so. Those of us who are in our forties went to college without computers of any kind, without the Internet, without cell phones, without Google, without GPS ... and the list goes on.

It was not until the mid '80s that computers began to be commercialized, moving from big companies, government institutions, and colleges and universities to our offices and homes. That was just twenty-five years ago. It was not until the '90s that the transformation from desktop to laptop took place and cell phones began to make their way into our culture. That was just twenty years ago. It was not until the mid-'90s that the dot-coms burst onto the scene, leveraging the Internet. That was just fifteen years ago. And it was not until the last ten years that two major shifts occurred: The first was the abundance of devices all over the world—whether cell phones, computers—all smaller, cheaper, and able to do more each year than the previous year. The second was the world's largest migration to a single source—the Internet. The accessibility to the Internet from all those aforementioned devices has created literally a new virtual world where people can do just about anything from anywhere. This *just* happened! We are still sorting through it. It is of tremendous importance that we understand it and leverage it. Those who do will be best prepared for the EPowered world we will be discussing in the later chapters.

Technological advances are transforming our sense of what is possible, both at work and in our personal lives. The pace of technological change is increasing constantly. Innovation and development of as-yet-unseen technologies make it hazardous to predict what will happen beyond the next ten years. On New Year's Eve and New Year's Day 2007–2008, mobile phone users around the world sent a record-breaking 43 billion text messages,

30 percent more than the previous year. The fifty million mobile subscribers in the Philippines sent the highest number: an astonishing 1.39 billion text messages.[26] Clearly, we can expect that change will continue to occur at an exponential rate for a long time to come.

Advances in technology have produced changes that we now take for granted. It is easy to forget that these changes would have been reserved to the realm of science fiction not that many years ago. Technology is something we have come to expect. Today, 76 percent of frequent fliers would change their airline to have Wi-Fi, and 55 percent would change their flight by a full day to have access to the technology. Also, 71 percent of fliers would rather have wi-fi access than meal service. Ninety-four percent agree that in-flight wi-fi is the best thing airlines have done in the last three years.[27]

Consider what has happened to the pace of communication over a short period of time. It used to take up to ten days to send a letter to a foreign destination and another ten to receive a response. Thanks to cell phones and low-cost technologies like Skype, what used to take up to a month of "snail mail" exchanges to complete is now taken care of in seconds, any time.

> *A key skill for future leaders will be leading virtually. The skills that go along with leading virtually include not only comfort with technology but an ability to leverage technology efficiently (and within budget) to manage virtual teams well. The virtual nature of teams is bringing a changing dynamic to building and managing relationships. Trust looks different in a virtual world, and it is much easier to feel disconnected with a virtual team—it takes more time to build a relationship with a virtual team.*

—Todd Harrison, director of leadership and
associate development, WellPoint

Instant communication online and via mobile devices is having a worldwide cultural impact, affecting even the world's social order and politics. It was once possible for a government to clamp down on communications devices and access to information. This is no longer true. The social unrest in Iran arising from the elections of 2009 illustrates how connectivity is making it all but impossible for any government to control the flow of information. Access to the Internet and applications like Twitter provided the people of Iran with constant access to each other and to the world.

The Influence of Technology on the Workplace

The foundation has been laid for a tectonic shift in the workplace. A number of forces in play will radically change how we think about work and what we actually do.

> *The pace of technological change will have an effect on the pace of business. A saying we have at Black & Decker is "be brief, be bright, and be gone," meaning that time is at a premium these days, so you should state your point succinctly, be able to come up with alternative solutions, and then move on to the next thing.*

—Bob Zierk, VP of human resources,
Black & Decker

According to McKinsey & Co., nearly 85 percent of new jobs created between 1998 and 2006 involved complex knowledge work, like problem solving and concocting corporate strategy. The growing role of technology at work will increasingly change the focus of work. Over the next seven years, the number of jobs in the information technology sector is expected to swell 24 percent—a figure more than twice the overall job growth rate.

> *We are entering an era of transparency where we are all producers. Printed media and corporate communications are moving toward instantaneous commentary, and that requires forethought of presentation. That presentation must be authentic, because the audience has access to more information, so it must be truthful.*
>
> —Effenus Henderson, chief diversity officer,
> Weyerhaeuser

We have become interconnected and will continue to be, all leveraged by very powerful collaborative technologies—both on the application side (iPhone's ad: there's an app for everything) and on the hardware side (the number of devices that are connected to each other is already approaching fifteen billion). We cannot underscore enough the impact of this technology on human behavior, on performance, and on business. For those of us focused on helping the workforce perform at higher levels, we simply cannot ignore this. At a large Fortune 100 company, a top executive recently said that "we're simply not ready for technology to govern our interactions ... and that scares me." And he was not talking about using computers or cell phones; these are already archaic by some standards. He was talking about the e world and the collaborative technologies that foster accessibility to that collective human knowledge critical for making better decisions, in real time, from anywhere—no matter the topic.

"If I had to pick just one area to focus on development, I would recommend that professionals develop their comfort with technology. A comfort with and ability to use technology will allow people to extract the information they need and convert it into knowledge.

—Linda Worden, director of training and organizational development, MeadWestvaco Corporation

Rapid, Transformative Change

We've become accustomed to change that is occurring at an exponential rate. The world has been transformed within a single generation. If someone were transported from the world we knew in the 1970s, that person would think that he or she had landed in some distant future. Even though the changes took place over less than twenty-five years or so, these changes are so dramatic that they would make the future all but unrecognizable.

Twenty-five years ago, the idea of doing an online search for information was unheard-of. With the development of the first Web sites and search engines in the '90s, instantaneous access to unlimited information rapidly became a reality. By 2007, there were over 31 billion searches on Google every month.[28] This is a marked increase from just the year before, when the monthly average was "only" 2.7 billion searches.

We see a similar steep growth pattern in the use of text messages. The very first commercial text message was sent in December 1992. By 2007, we saw a total of 363 billion messages, followed by more than one trillion messages in 2008. Today, 4.1 billion text messages are being sent *daily,* which is twice as many as in 2008. This is coming from about 276 million wireless users.[29]

The adoption of new technological devices and other services shows a similar pattern of exponential change. One measure is how long it takes a device or application to reach a market of more than fifty million people. It took the radio thirty-eight years to reach that many people. Television took thirteen years. But the adoption of new technology accelerated. The Internet reached the fifty-million-user mark in just four years. The iPod took only three years to sell as many units, and Facebook surpassed fifty million users in less than two years. At the time of this writing, if Facebook were a nation, it would now be the fifth-largest country in the world.[30]

In 1984, there were only a thousand devices connected to what was going to become known as the Internet. In 1992, that number exceeded one million. Again, exponential growth is seen, with more than six hundred million devices on the Internet in 2006. By 2008, that number exceeded one billion devices online. By as early as next year, that number is expected to reach more than fourteen billion—which means that there will be twice as many devices connected to the Internet as there are people on the entire planet.

Through keyword-driven Internet research using search engines like Google, millions of people worldwide have easy and instant access to a vast and diverse amount of online information. Compared with encyclopedias and traditional libraries, the Internet has enabled a sudden and extreme decentralization of information and data. [31]

Mobile telephones, data cards, handheld game consoles, and cellular routers are all devices that allow users to connect to the Internet. All that is required is wireless access to the Internet, a service that is constantly being upgraded and expanded while it is also getting cheaper. This is producing a level of universal connectivity that is only now beginning to be fully understood and deployed to our advantage.

Today, more than any other time in the history of mankind, we are awash in information. Through the e world, we can access an unheard-of volume of information instantly. Let's put that in perspective. It is estimated that a single week of the *New York Times* contains more information than someone who lived in the eighteenth century was likely to encounter in an entire lifetime.

Information is accumulating at an astonishing rate. It has been estimated that 161 exabytes (an exabyte is a quintillion bytes) of data was created in 2006 and that number will soar to 988 exabytes by 2010. Of that, more than four exabytes is unique and new information. How much is an exabyte? Well, 161 exabytes is *three million times* the amount of information contained in all the books ever written, and four exabytes is more information than has been uniquely generated in the previous five thousand years.[32]

The growth of information and advances in technology are presenting challenges to educators and business leaders who must adapt to keep pace. The amount of technical information is doubling every two years. In fact, students working on a four-year degree may soon find themselves in the unheard-of position of discovering that what they learned in their first year of study is already outdated by the third year of their training.

Access to information defines how we live and work today. As detailed in a groundbreaking work by Friedman, *The World is Flat*, the lowering of trade and political barriers and the revolutionary advances in technology have made it possible that we can now do business with anyone, anywhere, instantaneously.[33] So, technology has flattened the world and shattered barriers.

The twentieth century is often referred to as the American century. The twenty-first century is almost certainly going to become known as the global century. It will be marked by a revolution in how we think about and do business. Business will no longer be driven solely by giant corporations. Connectivity and the easy availability of wide spread technologies will make it possible for individuals and small businesses to flourish in the markeplace.

The Changing Workplace

The nature of work—and the workplace—is changing. In 1991, less than half of the jobs that existed required a skilled laborer. Today, the top ten jobs most in demand didn't even exist in 2004.[34] As the former U.S. Secretary of Education Richard Riley put it, "We are currently preparing students for jobs that don't yet exist, using technologies that haven't been invented, in order to solve problems we don't even know are problems yet."[35]

Changes are affecting what people used to think of as a steady career path. The baby boomer generation experienced an average of 10.8 jobs by the age of forty-two.[36] We can expect today's learners to double that, on average. Even now, one in four workers has been with his or her current employer for less than a year, and one in two workers has been with the current employer for less than five years.[37]

Not long ago, we could access the latest technology only at work. Access was expensive and well beyond the reach of the individual user. Today's technological devices and applications are so easily available and affordable to Americans that they have become a staple of modern life. Given the ease of access to

The Global Marketplace

It is necessary to take a quick look at demographics to truly grasp the opportunities in front of us in a global marketplace:

Population
In July 2009, the population of United States was estimated to be about 305 million people. China, on the other hand, contains 1,331,650,000 people, while India has 1,165,970,000 people.

Ability to speak English
At least for the near future, English is the language of business. China is soon to become the world's leader in terms of numbers of people who speak English. India ranks third, with more than ninety million people who speak English, followed by Nigeria with seventy-nine million.

Education and intelligence
In 2006, the total number of college graduates in the United States was 1.3 million. China had 3.3 million graduates, while India came in second with 3.1 million. The 25 percent of the population of India with the highest IQs is larger than the population of the entire United States.

These figures illustrate two compelling findings:
- Competition for leadership in business is truly international in scope.
- In a connected world, the opportunities for collaborative creativity and productivity are no longer defined by national boundaries.

information in our personal lives, it could even be argued that people are more efficient outside of work than they are at work.

Consider this story of one family; they discovered on a Sunday afternoon that their five-year-old had a small but growing rash on the back of her shoulder. Because both parents worked, that in effect meant that one of them was going to have to take the following day (Monday) off from work to take the child to the doctor. If you are a parent, you know the ordeal well. The wife went online to WebMD and, after a short search, found a picture of the same kind of rash and symptoms that affected the little girl. The Web site recommended an over-the-counter cream, which the mother promptly bought from a pharmacy down the road. On Monday morning, the rash was gone. This is just one example of how powerful an impact on our social culture and life technology has had, and just how efficient we have become. Or, rather, how EPowered we have become. Now, how many places of work allow their employees to be this resourceful?

> *Societal and technological changes have taken place, and we find ourselves at an inflection point. The opportunity now exists in social-interactive technologies.*
>
> —Michelle Marquard, Fortune 100
> Information Technology Company

This change is driven by new technologies, and it is causing a divide in the way people work. We are leading dichotomous lives. We live one way outside of work, where we are self-sufficient in unprecedented ways and the only barriers are in the beholder. Yet we work in a whole different way—bureaucracy, systems, processes, and even people constantly inhibit, either explicitly or implicitly, the ability of professionals to function as effectively at work as they do outside of work. Ironically, the workplace has become one of the most inefficient places to work. How many of you have said, "Gosh, I get so much more done at home"?

A second dichotomy comes from the age at which we became accustomed to these technologies. On one side of the divide, we have digital immigrants. On the other, we have digital natives.[38] Digital immigrants were trained to work with technology. They adapted their processes and work habits to include technology later in life. They include Generation X and the boomers. Digital natives have learned, from early on, to work with just technology. They do not need to "adapt" to new technologies and new ways of working, because the digital age is something they have grown up with and have always been accustomed to. The pace of change we see doesn't necessarily seem exponential to them—it's normal. These two groups cannot be more different in their expectations and use of technology.

A challenge for senior management is to understand what is needed to integrate technological innovations in their companies. All too often, investments in technology are made without the necessary concurrent enterprise-wide training, monitoring, and measurement systems. What is also lacking is a coherent vision, shared throughout the organization, that creates the proper context for the integration of new technologies into the life and operations of the organization. Some technological innovations go to the heart of an organization's way of getting things done and cannot be relegated to the information systems or operations departments. Rather, leaders must be seen as sourcing and supporting fundamental shifts in the practices and standards of their organizations.

Today, we have to deal with questions such as, "How do I best connect with someone on the other side of the world who works different hours?" "How do I hold people accountable for outcomes when I am not physically there?" "How can you leverage capabilities from every corner of the globe and not be limited by the structure of your organization?" "How do I give people enough strategic direction, when there are so many things that can change their path?"

—Jane Luciano, VP of global learning and
organization development,
Bristol-Myers Squibb

Organizations that eliminate these dichotomies and enable employees to be just as empowered at work as they are in life are clearly going to attract and retain the best talent. The companies that are the most successful in adopting innovations in technology are the ones in which workers can make decisions at work the same way that they make them at home. They can access information and learning points and communicate with others at the time that they need to. Companies are beginning to recognize that a workplace is no longer about furniture. In fact, a workplace without boundaries is already a reality for many people. This is a change that is being driven by innovation in communication, connectivity, and how we do business. The physical office is expected to remain an important node in our network of interactions, but businesses are coming to the realization that they can no longer afford to warehouse employees in the traditional way.

It is already happening. Companies like Sun Microsystems are leading the way. For seven years, Sun has been working on a program to take advantage of the company's own technology and retool the way employees approach their work. A project called Open Work is producing dramatic results. Operating from the premise that warehousing employees is financially unfeasible and is not conducive to flexibility and collaboration, many of Sun's employees now have no assigned office space in a fixed location. They work *when* they want to work and *where* they want to work. In pursuit of a workforce that is flexible, agile, and adaptive, Sun has already seen returns in the form of $387 million in savings over the past six years.[39] This is a great example of EPowerment.

> *Sun is a networking company. Our tagline is "the network is the computer." We believe it's possible for people to connect and do their work anyplace on the planet. We have 67 percent of our people working from home. We have developed best practices around working virtually. We provide all the tools and processes that people need to collaborate anywhere on the planet.*
>
> —Karie Willyerd, CLO, Sun Microsystems

Over seventeen million Americans worked from home at least one day a month in 2008. That's an increase of 39 percent over 2006 and 74 percent over 2005.[40] However, working remotely causes 243 percent more workplace relationship problems (e.g., lack of trust and misrepresentation of information) than working in the same place, according to new research by corporate training consultants VitalSmarts. Difficulties between long-distance colleagues are not only more common, but they're harder to fix. Fifty-four percent of survey respondents said that, when problems crop up with local coworkers, they tend to last a few days. When asked about relationships with remote colleagues, the highest number, 35 percent, said that problems last a few weeks.[41] But this won't stop us from working remotely. It simply means we'll have to work to adapt to the new situation. This only intensifies the need for EPowerment.

To illustrate the changes that are taking place and that require us to adapt our current style of working, consider the technological innovations that changed our lives between 2008 and 2009. Here are several things you can do now, that you couldn't just a mere two years ago:[42]

- **Everything on the go.** Thanks to the iPhone and other new cellular products, computing is now free of the desktop and even the laptop. E-mail and Web searches are even more accessible than ever before.
- **Search through all e-mail.** Google now makes it possible to save up to twenty-five gigabytes of e-mail. A newly developed search engine makes it possible to quickly retrieve targeted e-mail messages out of this wealth of information.
- **Chat with customers and partners in any language.** Thanks to new instantaneous translation technology, it is now possible to chat with people without concern about the barrier of differing languages. This is a boon in today's global marketplace.
- **Organize all business travel through e-mail.** A new technology allows busy business travelers to manage all business itineraries through e-mail. The program even updates calendars.
- **Collaborate simply and securely online.** By using Google applications, we can now collaborate online without concern about security. This can even be done from a handheld device, because the online

application frees people from the need to have a variety of memory-consuming applications stored on their devices.

- **Broad use of additional applications.** Cloud computing has literally unchained us from our desks. Coupled with a wide variety of applications, forms, online presentations, and a wide variety of other services, we are literally able to do business at any time, from any place.

All these capacities became available over the course of just two short years—yet more evidence that exponential change is upon us with untold other advances surely to arrive in the future.

Impact of Technology on Business Leadership

It is amazing how technology is often positioned as an "unacceptable substitute" for the "human touch." Granted, there are missing elements in the electronic forms of communication but technology is here to stay. A recent study found that over 70 percent of workplace communication is electronic. In lieu of debating the pros and cons of each of the modes of working, the use of technology and the human touch need to coexist. Those who take full advantage of optimizing this coexistence are likely to outperform those who don't.

In 2010 and beyond, every leader—and that now means *everyone*—is able to connect to new *people, communities,* and *knowledge sources* in unprecedented ways. Given access to this wealth of knowledge, broad implementation of online applications, and instant connectivity, there should be no excuse for mediocre decision-making. No leader should be reinventing the wheel, duplicating mistakes, or not leveraging lessons learned.

Organizations only serve themselves better by EPowering their employees through accessibility to these sources of knowledge.

Technology alone won't get the job done. Giving a hunter the most sophisticated gun could be quite counter-productive if the hunter does not know how to use the gun or if the hunter does not have the courage to use it. This is where emotional intelligence, the core of every human being, comes to play. This is the second "e" of EPowerment. Adaptability, collaboration, and high performance, enabled by the fundamental shifts driven by technology and the e world will require an even more judicious deployment of emotional intelligence. Let us now discuss why EQ is more relevant now than ever.

Summary and Key Points

- Technological shifts have changed life and work in recent years:
  - Mass availability of devices with mobile Internet capabilities.
  - Migration of data, people, and interactions to a single source, the Internet.
- Interconnectedness has led to instant communication:
  - Enabling the growth of a global economy.
  - Technology facilitates entrepreneurship and small to mid-sized businesses.
- The pace of change is much faster than we have ever seen before.
- Data and knowledge exist in abundance—perhaps overabundance.
- The gap is growing between the way we access information, communicate with others, and make decisions at home and at work.
- Integrating innovation and harnessing the power for performance is difficult because it requires behavioral adaptation.
- Adapting to rapid change will be a challenge for organizations, especially as they exist now.

Chapter 3
Emotional Intelligence—EQ

Human memory is not only logical but also emotional. It's not only explicit, but also implicit. We learn from our past experiences. If we made a decision in the past that worked out well, our brain is likely to overlook red flags when a similar situation comes up in the future. When we have more experience, we rely less on logic and more on gut instinct. Is that a good thing or a bad thing? It's a neutral process until your behavior is affected and that behavior is followed by consequences. This situation played out for William Smithburg, former chairman of Quaker Oats, with some major consequences. When making the decision to acquire Snapple, he was vividly reminded of Gatorade, Quaker's most successful deal. Snapple, like Gatorade, appeared to be a new drink company that could be improved with Quaker's marketing and management skills. But the similarities were superficial. Rather than creating value, this decision was ultimately destructive for Quaker. In fact, buying Snapple was Smithburg's worst deal.[43]

Doing business in the new economy will require leaders and teams to focus on developing new competencies. It is impossible to develop new ways of operating by relying on the old ways of doing business. The competency that lies at the heart of the new organization is *emotional intelligence* (EQ). While technology has given us many tools and changed our world, the final frontier of individual and organizational performance is determined by how emotionally intelligent we are. The amalgam of the two, the e world and EQ, is what EPowerment is all about.

End Game: Everyone is High Performing

The ultimate goal for individuals and organizations alike is to achieve maximum levels of performance. Given the powerful forces for change impacting the next ten years, it is helpful to reflect on what precedes, physiologically, high performance. What is happening in the individual that leads to that high performance?

Effective and timely decision-making is at the heart of good performance. To improve performance, we need to understand how to make better decisions.

Our level of performance is captured by our competencies.

Competencies are the things we know how to do and what we are good at—our capabilities. They are specific skills and abilities, such as delivering a great presentation, writing effectively, using active listening skills during communications, or knowing how to negotiate a sales deal. This is where the majority of performance management processes lie, built on the concept that competencies are the direct antecedent or predecessor to good decision making and high performance.

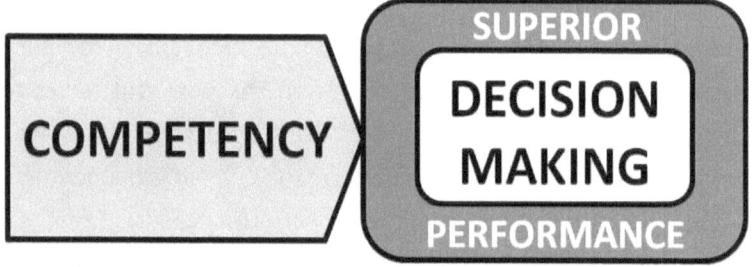

If you are good at something, you have a competency, which allows you to perform well in that specific area. Conversely, if you are not good at something, then you are likely to not perform well. Competencies can be innate or they can be acquired through learning.

Preceding our competencies are our behaviors. The acceptability of most behaviors is largely dependent on the culture of the organization.

Behaviors include our day-to-day activities that determine where we focus our time and where we focus our energies. All of us know people who have mastered specific competencies. They may be good at speaking, putting together certain tasks at work, or solving certain kinds of problems. But many of these folks exhibit behaviors that set them back. These inadequate or inappropriate behaviors dilute their competencies, which in turn compromise their ability to perform at high levels. So these people, although full of potential, let their innate talent go to waste because they do not harness it, do not tie to a passion, or do not put in the effort and the practice that it takes to be truly great.

Thirty years ago, it may have been inappropriate for a manager to discuss these behaviors with an employee, but today it is accepted protocol. If behaviors interfere with effectiveness on the job, they must be addressed in coaching and performance management.

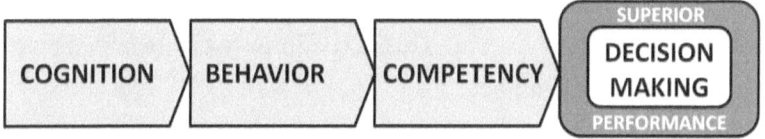

Cognition precedes behavior. Slightly oversimplifying this concept, cognition refers to one's intellectual capacities, thoughts, knowledge, and memories. This is the rational part of our brain. In effect, it is our ability to take data points, weave them together in some cogent manner, and reach a conclusion that dictates, consciously or subconsciously, what behavior to exhibit. Our cognitions dictate the competency manifested, subsequently determining our level of performance. If your thinking leads to the wrong conclusion, the rest of the steps get compromised, no matter how competent you and your behavior may be.

What finally precedes cognition in this physiological sequence to high performance is one's EQ.

To illustrate this process with a practical example, consider the aforementioned hunter with the new gun. If a hunter is trained in the competencies required to handle the new gun, he has the skills to outperform someone who has not had that training. This is the impact our skills, abilities, and competencies can have on our performance. Similarly, professional development has focused on developing competencies to address identified deficiencies or to pursue career paths that require certain designated competencies.

Now consider a well-trained hunter who is unaware of the impact of his cell phone use on the other hunters or even the prey. It does not matter how good he is, his incongruent behavior has compromised his ability to make the hunt successful for both himself and his colleagues. This is the impact our behaviors can have on our performance.

Now let's say the hunter is well-trained on the new gun and has wonderful behaviors. But in his mind, he misinterpreted certain signals from his friends or the environment he was in. He thought he was aiming at his target, when in reality it was simply a tree. His behaviors and performance are then based on this flawed assumption, and his goal is not reached. What happened here? His erroneous thinking has led to an error in judgment. No matter how good his training and behaviors were, performance was compromised due to his faulty cognition.

Next, we have emotions. What if the hunter felt an imminent threat, imagined or real? For example, what if one of his friends made a joke about his shoes. Unbeknownst to the friend, the comment triggered a negative memory for the hunter. The hunter's emotions have set off an alarm and may affect his thinking and behavior—both now far removed from the task at hand of hunting. No matter how smart the hunter is or how great his

What is Emotional Intelligence?

EQ is composed of two broad areas – your relationship with yourself (intrapersonal) and others (interpersonal). Intrapersonal intelligence is made up of Self-Awareness, Self-Regulation, and Motivation. Interpersonal intelligence is made up of Empathy and Social Skills.

Self-Regulation: An important factor in the effectiveness of expressing emotions is how we do it. Yelling, cursing, and throwing things at someone, for example, is not the most effective way to communicate anger. Mentors help mentees to determine the best way to manage and appropriately express emotions in the workplace.

Motivation: Determining professional goals is an integral component of becoming and staying motivated. Listening to others' experiences can be a powerful trigger for your own motivation, fueling your learning experience.

Social Skills: Good communication skills are the key to more effective social interaction. Responding well to others' emotions allows for an improved ability to make strong, lasting connections with people.

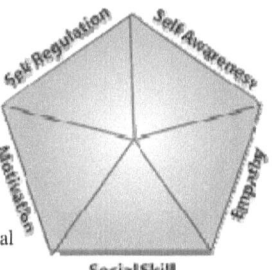

Self-Awareness: Words and actions have an impact on others, and in the business world this directly translates into success. The more you understand yourself, the more you can improve the impact you have on others. With the help of a mentor, users work on building self-confidence and self-esteem. With increased confidence comes the ease of expressing feelings.

Empathy: One way to increase your connection with other people is by trying to put yourself in their shoes. By practicing this in the workplace, you can put empathy in action. It is by seeing the world through another's eyes that we can change our behaviors, thoughts, and actions.

IQ versus EQ

EQ and IQ are independent -- unrelated to each other even though both are important to performance. Their role in high performance can be explained through a compensatory model. As IQ decreases, the role of EQ in high-level performance becomes even more important. While IQ is best suited for tasks where only cognition is important, our EQ is intended for navigating social situations, which are prevalent everywhere. Today's jobs demand high levels of *both* IQ and EQ. This foundational competency is the basis for many of the best decisions, the most dynamic and profitable organizations, and the most satisfying lives.

"In hard times, the soft stuff often goes away. But emotional intelligence, it turns out, isn't so soft. If emotional obliviousness jeopardizes your ability to perform, fend off aggressors, or be compassionate in a crisis, no amount of attention to the bottom line (IQ) will protect your career. Emotional intelligence isn't a luxury tool you can dispense with in tough times. It's a basic tool that, deployed with finesse, is the key to professional success."

-The Harvard Business Review, April 2003

competencies are, at least in the short-term, the hunter's ability to perform at a high level is compromised. This is the power of emotions and the relevance of emotional intelligence to high performance. Not only does it come first, it also trumps all the other components necessary to perform the task at hand. This is why we see seemingly very good and competent people at work reacting in dysfunctional ways when they feel threatened, especially during periods of high stress.

As illustrated, EQ refers to a body of personal characteristics and social abilities that are closely tied to success in both our professional and personal lives. While we can expect our understanding of EQ to continue to evolve as it is studied, EQ is here to stay. It continues to gain prominence in both academia and the corporate world. There is reason to believe that, unlike so many other concepts in the human capital space that have come and gone in recent years, EQ has the potential to stay and grow in acceptance and practice. Whereas previous human capital trends have focused on key competencies, and important ones at that, EQ lays the foundation for those competencies.

In addition to being a core and foundational competency, EQ captures the entirety of who *you are as an individual*—as opposed to who you may be at work or at a certain function or in a certain place with certain people. As a result, the impact of improving your EQ can and does easily translate to almost all parts of your life and relationships.

Whereas most workplace professional development concepts focus on an individual *with* others, EQ focuses on that individual *and* others. Having a great relationship with someone else, whoever that person may be (a coworker, a boss, a spouse, etc.) is the direct result of having a good relationship with yourself—and not vice versa. Kevin Henry, chief HR officer, integrates EQ with his work at Coca-Cola Bottling Consolidated Co., "The foundation of trust comes from a focus on leading, with the main objective being building relationships on a personal basis."

Emotional competence is essential in an environment requiring people to deal with constantly changing roles and to invent new ways of getting things done. Imagine people working at home,

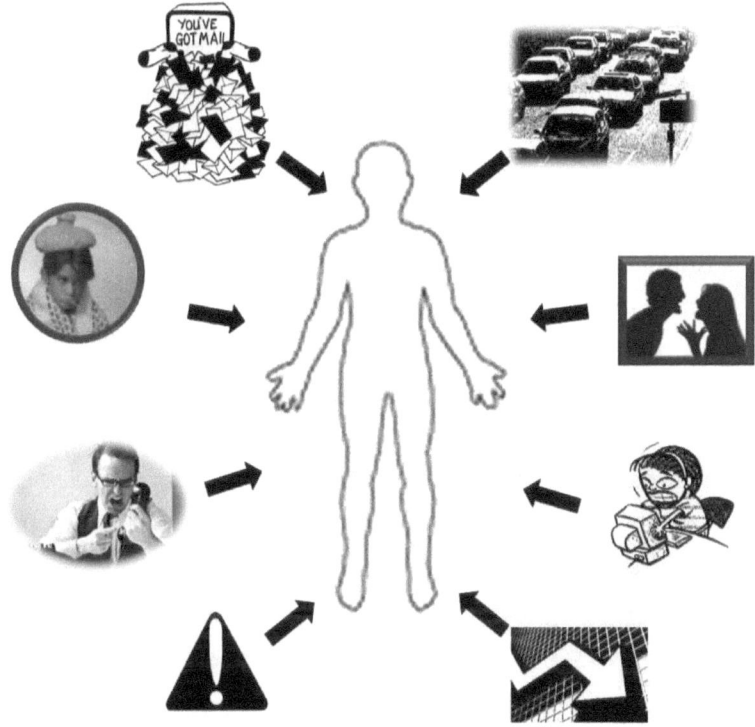

sharing positions, and moving from project to project. The ability to manage ourselves and our relationships becomes even more critical than it is today.

For example, companies have been talking about teamwork for almost two decades. The connection between how employees get along with people at work and with people in their personal lives is not often made. EQ is about *each individual*, the real and whole person. Awareness of emotional state and how it affects a person's behavior is transferable to all dimensions of life.

The Role of Emotional Competence

We are a product of the interaction of our genetically determined predispositions and the accumulation of our daily experiences. This combination is so unique that no two people are the same. Even genetically identical twins will demonstrate different behaviors as a result of different experiences. Though we cannot change our genetics or control what happens to us, we can change the impact of our experiences. We can also leverage our talents and abilities and compensate for our weaknesses.

Similarly, in the workplace, our success is determined by a combination of emotional intelligence, technical skills, and cognitive abilities. Enhancing your cognitive abilities, behaviors, and competencies will only get you so far. A growing body of research has demonstrated that EQ accounts for up to 80 percent of the variance in differentiating star performers from their peers. That means that, given a baseline of equal intellectual ability and technical skill, EQ is that secret ingredient that decides whose performance will stand out from that of their peers.

This is especially true today. In this decade, the best work is done collaboratively, by teams, or by groups of people. An individual with the highest IQ cannot and will not outperform a team composed of individuals with mediocre IQ but high EQ. This is because a team can get more done and can collaborate more effectively. But the same process that enables that excellence can also destroy it.

Over the course of a work day, unsolicited negative experiences occur. No one wakes up in the morning wishing for negative experiences to occur; we don't seek out or intend for them to happen to us. They occur as a natural part of life and we often have little control over them. These negative experiences might then produce negative emotions. The potential of these negative emotions to take over our brains and our bodies, and subsequently negatively impact our performance, is grossly underestimated.

Negative experiences are emotional disablers. Just as everyone is unique, everyone has unique trigger events that can act as emotional disablers. The negative emotions that result release stress hormones. These negative experiences, which happen to all of us whether we want them to or not, affect not only *what we think* and *how we behave* the rest of the day, but also our physical state. This is a physiological reaction that has physical effects:

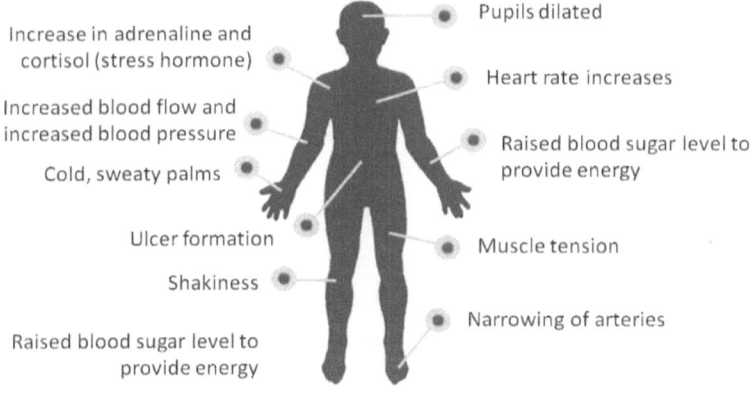

Increase in adrenaline and cortisol (stress hormone)

Increased blood flow and increased blood pressure

Cold, sweaty palms

Ulcer formation

Shakiness

Raised blood sugar level to provide energy

Pupils dilated

Heart rate increases

Raised blood sugar level to provide energy

Muscle tension

Narrowing of arteries

Our reactions to stress can result in a physically and emotionally disabled state. How is it possible to perform at a high level in such a state? How many days have you operated this way? How many days have your employees operated this way? What is the impact of the loss of all that time where collaboration was needed and decisions were being made? What if we knew how to manage emotions so that the impact of the negative experiences was minimized in such a way that performance was not compromised?

An average negative experience exerts physiological effects on one's body for approximately four hours (four hours is how long your system remains over-activated). So, if an employee gets an e-mail with negative undertones (real or imagined) from a boss or a fellow employee, then for up to four hours, the employee's optimal performance is compromised. That employee is emotionally disabled for four hours. Let's say that the average worker has two negative experiences a day (perhaps someone cut him off in traffic on his way to work, for example), then essentially, that employee will be underperforming (disabled) for the rest of the day, assuming an eight-hour workday. There could not be a more impressive business case for emotional intelligence than this. If working professionals specifically, and humans beings in general, do not appreciate the power of their own emotions and the impact they have, both positively and negatively, on their performance, then a great deal of time and money is wasted each day in disengagement and underperformance.

The negative experiences are not inherently bad. It is our perception that makes them so. A stressful, alerted state is not necessarily debilitating either. It can enhance performance if it doesn't incapacitate us first! In fact, too little stress can be just as damaging to performance as an overload of stress. This is the ultimate power of EQ: harnessing emotions rather than falling victim to them.

Now, what if a manager or leader orchestrates a positive experience for his or her staff? Could the positive endorphins also stay in the human body for a period of time to either dilute the negative experiences already in existence or enhance the overall body? Of course! It is this ability to recognize and apply emotional acumen that is emotional intelligence.

Just as we experience negative emotions every day, we also

experience positive ones, what we call emotional enablers. These are activities that provide us with the kinds of physical and emotional attributes shown below.

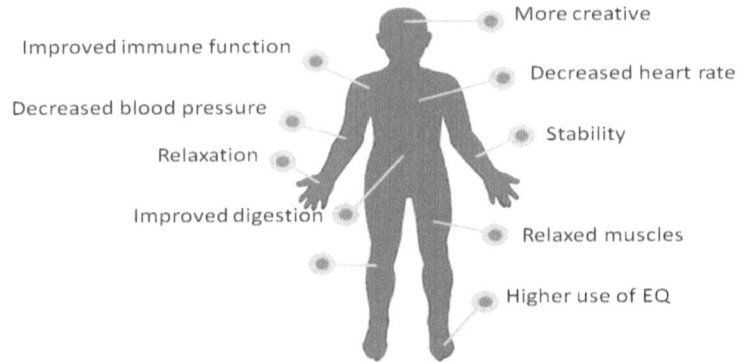

How powerful could we be if, every time that we experienced negative emotions, we could consciously call forth emotional enablers to counteract the emotional disablers? Do you know people who, in the midst of chaos, stand out calm and collected, orchestrating their own behavior and those of others to resolve the issue? You can do it too. In fact, you can do it for people around you.

Think of a metaphoric emotional thermometer that you can use to measure both your own emotional temperature and that of your team. If you had a list of emotional enablers, you could deploy them when the temperature reached a point where no one could be productive. Having a list of emotional enablers for yourself is highly recommended so you can regulate your own state. Being aware of emotional disablers as incompatible with high performance is critical. Avoiding them altogether or making sure they are addressed very quickly when they occur is the power of emotional intelligence. It should be clear now why this is such a powerful component of empowerment.

Personal Growth Tip:
Make Two Lists

Make a list of **emotional enablers**. Recall that emotional enablers are the people, situations, trinkets, or activities that make you feel better. Use the positivity they bring to lift your mood and help you achieve higher performance in situations your emotions take over.

Make a list of **emotional disablers**. Recall that emotional disablers are the people, situations, or activities that quickly turn your mood sour. Avoid these when you are already stressed, working on a deadline, or need to be performing at your best.

EQ and Performance

Given a baseline set of technical skills and IQ, imagine your potential with a higher level of EQ. For example, athletics is the ultimate arena for performance. In competitive golf, it takes about four and a half hours to play a round, but the actual amount of time spent hitting a shot is less than five minutes. Thus, the overwhelming majority of a competitive golfer's time is really spent with his or her own thoughts and emotions. In a non-reactionary sport like golf, the single most important aspect of competitive advantage is the golfer's ability to manage his or her emotions, especially after a bad shot.

In sports, where high performance can be viewed and measured instantly, the results are right there in front of everyone. In the end, you win or you lose; you performed your best, you were mediocre, or you played horribly. Such results are quite immediate. The better players are always those who seem to thrive under pressure. They play well when it counts, which is usually when the game is on the line.

Imagine a basketball player who has one second left and is on the free throw line. He has to make the free throw to win for his team. The only difference between this shot and countless others is timing—and the anxiety associated with that timing. The sizes of the ball and the basket, and the distance to the rim have not changed at all. What has changed is the emotions that the player is experiencing.

Our lives are filled with emotional disablers. Emotional intelligence is one of the more defining, yet underrated, components of performance—both in athletics and in the workplace. Specifically, the conscious use of emotional enablers has the potential to make the greatest impact. The one major difference is that, unlike performance in sports, it is easier to hide or disguise performance at work. The results are rarely visible to everyone, often times they not even measured, and in some cases, they are not even understood. The line between busy activity and results is often blurred in the workplace.

Granted, the workplace does not have a shot clock or an audience watching our every play, but we do have performance metrics we are expected to hit—either those we set ourselves or those our bosses or companies have established for us. For example, if you're in sales, you must have a target or quota that you need to meet. Performance EQ translates well into the workplace—it is your ability to perform under the gun that also defines your success. Again, EQ is the centerpiece of this puzzle as well.

Leaders with high EQ know that empathy creates a positive impact through listening and engagement, even when no definitive outcome or action item is reached. Listening is yet another emotional enabler. Emotional intelligence has never been more relevant to leadership than it is today. View each person you come in contact with this week as a person that you have the ability to inspire, motivate, listen to, and learn from. You can emotionally enable anyone. Know that when your activated sympathetic nervous system triggers fight-or-flight mode, it is greatly compromising innovation and creativity when it is needed most. Your heart beats faster to pump increased oxygen, adrenaline, and sugar into your bloodstream, and only good healthy, positive interaction can dilute that activity.

Research shows it takes five positive experiences (enablers) to dilute a negative one (disabler).[44] It takes five interactions where you are smiling, laughing, praising, or connecting to make up for a time where you have criticized, frowned, or otherwise unintentionally upset your relationship. Be one of those five emotional enablers for everyone you come into contact with this week.

Food Lion, LLC agrees with this model. Its model emphasizes that both accountability and relatedness are needed to achieve high performance. Susan Richter, director of human resources, says, "In our old model, the way we used to do things, the system has rewarded the demanding driver. But the problem with that perspective is that when a manager playing the role of the demanding driver walks out the door, the results stop. Now we are shifting to making a difference. If you know more about the person and relate to them, and you have provided context for the goals, you can make a difference in leadership of not only that individual but the entire team."

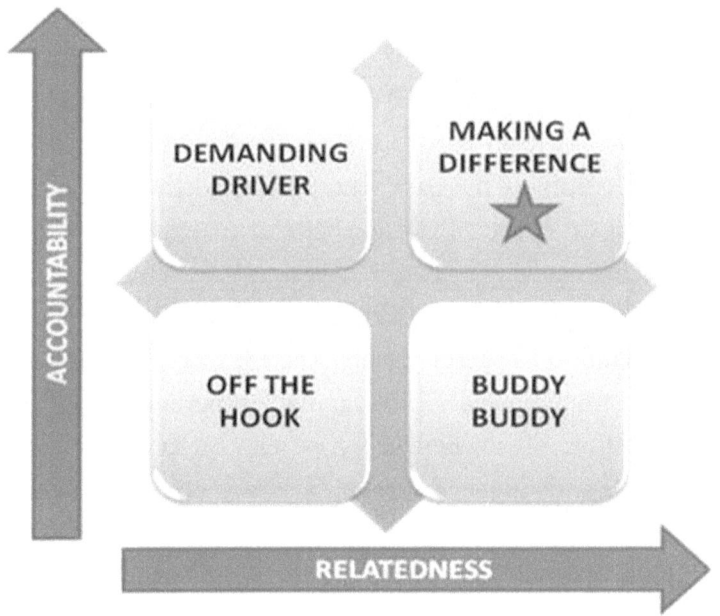

Emotional Relativity and Maintaining Emotional Balance

Two friends go hiking in a large park. Mary trips and breaks her arm during the hike. Beth also trips, but only has a minor cut on her arm. Clearly, Mary has a more traumatic experience and is in more pain. Let's fast forward and say that both of them decide to go hiking again a year later. Again, they both trip. But this time, the experience is reversed. Mary scratches her arm and Beth breaks her arm. It is plausible to assume that Mary, after having broken her arm before and experienced that trauma, merely brushes off the scratch and does not think twice about it. After all, she has been through much worse in the past. For Beth, however, who had only experienced a scratch before, the breaking of the arm is quite traumatic, since it was so much more painful than a scratch.

As Mary and Beth illustrate, emotional experiences are relative—two people going through identical experiences will almost never have the same emotional response because the response is based on their previous experiences and how they processed events in the past. Those of us who have had more challenging experiences in life are better prepared than those who have had less challenging experiences simply because our scale for measuring the gravity of these experiences is so different. We have different emotional thermometers. There is an old saying, "Some of us learn from our experiences, and others never recover." Those who learn from their experiences have a far better opportunity to have significantly higher EQ than those who do not. So in effect, those who have had more traumatic experiences in their past also have more opportunity to have higher EQ than those who have not.

Consider the implications of this. Victims of all kinds are able to achieve higher degrees of success if they are able to convert their experiences into learning moments. They can convert their emotional disablers into enablers, which is one of the highest forms of transformation and EQ. This is quite a dramatic shift from the victim's paradigm, which blames others (rightfully so, in many cases) or hides behind difficult experiences for long periods of time.

Some people would rather be victimized than do the work necessary to take responsibility for how they feel. Others have been taught that their feelings are beyond their control, and they haven't yet developed the self-awareness that will help them see the linkage between their thoughts and their feelings. But the quality of our emotional life is determined by how we react to events and experiences.

As a leader, it can be incredibly powerful to have a sense

of your team members' past emotional experiences, what their thermometer is, as this knowledge can provide great clues to how much resilience they have and their mastery of EQ. This is very critical to understand and appreciate—not only when it comes to growing one's own EQ, but to understanding others' as well. We acknowledge that this may seem inappropriate, just as it was seemingly inappropriate to discuss behaviors at work a few decades ago. But for today and tomorrow, this is the key to understanding how EQ works and how it can contribute to high performance.

Our challenges and failures, whether at home or at work, are tremendous opportunities for learning and growing. It is during these trying times that our awareness is at a unique high. That situational awareness can produce significant new insights about ourselves, resulting in learning moments. But first, we must be open to learning something new during tough experiences. We must have a baseline of resilience to address these challenges head-on. In doing so, we are one step closer to achieving EPowerment.

Best Practices During Challenging Times
Dr. Izzy Justice

During the 2008–2009 recession, we went through a challenging time. Whenever you opened a newspaper, listened to a radio station, or watched the news, you heard of anxiety—driven by the malignant economy. The anxiety of the folks being laid off is unparalleled. Not only are people being laid off, they may have little savings and have no place to go, or they lack the means to provide for their families. In addition, survivors of layoffs are just as anxiety-stricken since the unspoken rule seems to be "adopt a low profile and do your job." At a time when there has never been a more dire need for ingenuity and collaboration in the workplace, everyone seems to be running for cover. They are emotionally disabled. In other words, EPowerment is most needed in these challenging times, yet this is a time when it is most compromised.

Too many leaders ignore workplace survivors, thinking that they should feel grateful to still have a job. But the survivors' world has been radically changed. They've suffered the significant losses of relationships with colleagues who meant much to them but who are no longer with the company. In addition, they may be adjusting to changes in roles and being asked to do more with less. In the background is the looming thought that maybe their jobs will be among the next to be cut. Helping people stay focused and productive in such insecure times takes a concerted effort on the part of leaders, who must be accessible, answer questions, provide what reassurance they can, and show authentic understanding for what people in their organizations are experiencing.

Management
Managers and leaders have to understand that this is the time to practice taking care of people and over communicating.

- *Notice.* Explore the emotional temperature of the room and the people in it. Realize that the lower the EQ reading on that temperature, the lower the performance you can expect.
- *Connect.* Try traditional practices such as MBWA (Manage By Wandering Around), brown bag lunches, weekly conferences calls, or staff meetings cascaded throughout the organization. Consider starting meetings with five minutes of discussion over how to support each other and your organization.

Merger and Restructuring
Once a merger is announced, the only people that get excited are the shareholders and top executives. Employees, middle managers, and even customers tend to get worried about how this will impact them. This is an emotionally disabling time. To ease this anxiety, the governing mantra should be two-fold:

- Take very good care of the folks leaving because it sends a powerful message to the folks staying.
- Over communicate with those staying. Make your message explicit, because implicit assumptions during a stressful time will naturally shift toward the negative.

Self-Leadership
Consider redecorating your office or your room or adding to what is in your wallet or in your cell phone—fill these places with meaningful items that can instantly take you to a great place for centering yourself, your mind, and your emotions. Your space is, after all, *your* space. And if it is a place where you need to perform your best, then surround it with everything you can possibly think of that can help you perform your best, help you feel EPowered!

Transforming our Experiences

The older we get, the more we succeed and fail at things in general—our sample size for validating what has worked and not worked has increased a great deal every year of our lives. In terms of emotional relativity, as we age, we create a stronger buffer as a result of processing our experiences. This buffer prepares us to deal with unexpected challenges and conflicts. Eventually we realize what is best quoted by Walt Kelley, "We have met the enemy and he is us."

One way to accelerate the development of your emotional competence is to ask yourself self-reflective questions and write out responses. You will be amazed at the results. In doing this, you are, in effect, diluting the powerful negative emotions of a challenge with logic and action taking. That rational approach then empowers you to feel positive emotions. You are employing emotional enablers.

Critical thinking is arguably one of the most arduous skills to teach in leadership and management development. Writing is one of the most powerful tools to employ in developing critical thinking. When we write, we have all kinds of emotions and thoughts swirling through our minds.

Write something substantive each day—perhaps you own a daily journal or blog that is for your private and personal use. You will see results and a marked improvement in critical thinking and higher EQ over the course of a relatively short period of time. In fact, President Lincoln was an avid writer, not necessarily because he loved to write, but because he found writing to be a profound thinking tool.

> *I have found to be very beneficial for me in my own leadership growth, as well as for students of my leadership development programs, the concept of journaling. The process of journaling is similar to*

keeping a "diary" of your day and then taking time periodically to reflect back on your experiences from a different emotional perspective. This has allowed me to have new and interesting insights into situations that were at the time "emotionally charged." This is consistent I believe with your premise that the act of writing and reflecting contributes to more emotionally intelligent outcomes. Journaling is a basic concept I learned as a young army lieutenant as part of my early leadership development experiences and is a fundamental part of the military leader development process.

—Todd Harrison, director of leadership and associate development, WellPoint

What is the connection between EQ and writing? Your ability to connect emotionally with yourself and others is enhanced by processing the emotions involved through writing. Let's say that you just had a conflict-laden interaction with a peer or boss. If there is no one around you whom you trust to process the experience with, try writing it out with some structure. Ask yourself, "Why did this occur?" and then answer that question with the possibilities you can come up with. Then ask follow-up questions about how things might go differently next time, what aspects of the situation you can control, and what you have learned from the experience.

Emotional intelligence is arguably the singular competency that can help both employees and employers get out of a funk faster. The ability to recognize emotions, to regulate them, to motivate the desired ones, and to harness them for high performance will be paramount. We submit that EQ has never been more relevant in the workplace than now, and for the foreseeable future.

The Power of Negative Experiences
Dr. Izzy Justice

Negative experiences are going to happen and most of them are out of our control. However, negative emotions are necessary for positive ones to exist. If you've never been sad, it is quite possible you've never been truly happy either. If you've ever had a great day or a great experience, it is likely because you can juxtapose that to previous days or previous experiences that perhaps were not so good. In other words, it is easy to read popular literature (mostly non-scientific) and begin to take matters out of context.

While I am not suggesting we proactively seek negative experiences, I am suggesting that we seek new and challenging experiences where the likelihood of failure is possible. We can embrace negative experiences rather than nonchalantly brushing them off for fear of "being too negative" or "dwelling on it."

In my third book, *Is Today the Day?*, I interviewed dozens of stage IV cancer patients. Almost all told me that they learned more from their mistakes in life than their successes and wished they had taken more risks. To learn from mistakes and figure out ways to make yourself and the world a better place is truly one of life's grandest opportunities. The rewards are incalculable and the resultant emotions are just priceless.

We should not confuse having a positive attitude with denying and avoiding learning from negative experiences. Whatever you feel is right. If you're sad and someone asks, "How are you?" concede that you are sad—with the expectation that it is an effort to make yourself better. Responding to the previous question with "Doing just great! How about you?" is not only deceiving and disingenuous, it is not necessary. I urge my readers to not throw the gift of negative experiences away. They happen every day whether we want them to or not. By simply questioning and dialoguing, we can probably find ways to make ourselves, others, and life better. This is the power of emotions.

Summary and Key Points

- Emotional Intelligence is a foundational competency, lying at the heart of all other skills that contribute to high performance.
- High performance is a consequence of making good decisions at the right time.
- Skills, smarts, and behaviors are important to high performance, but emotions can wreak havoc on that equation.
- Negative experiences physically transform your system, leaving you prone to making bad decisions and exhibiting poor behaviors.
- Have a list of emotional enablers for yourself and your team, and be aware of what emotional disablers are. Learn to recognize and use all.
- Life's negative experiences are a wonderful source for ultimate transformations.
- Emotional relativity determines why two people react differently to the same stressful event.
- Journaling is a way of developing perspective and expanding EQ.

Chapter 4
EPowerment

When he was CEO of Medtronic, a medical device company, Bill George saw a Medtronic catheter fail during an operation. When investigating the issue afterward, he found the sales representative had reported defects back to the company but never received feedback on progress made. The engineers of the product denied the possibility of faulty design. As the engineers saw it, their job was to create a widget and that was about it. They were too far removed from the use of that instrument to care about quality, customer experience, etc. This is despite the level of managerial support and values statements putting the customer first. George insisted that the engineers see the product, in use, in the field. It worked. The engineers were much more engaged in making a great product after that experience.[45]

As this story illustrates, accountability is an archaic way of getting to high performance. Performance measures are not the key motivators. This is not to say they are not good, but employees need to have an inherent, intrinsic passion for the vision, mission, and goals of the company. Empowerment can make that happen.

> *A friend new to leadership once asked me, "How do you control your team?" I explained to him that I have no interest in controlling my team; my goal is to inspire my team to accomplish our shared goals.*
>
> —Keith Passwater, regional vice president, central market group, WellPoint

The elements that attract people to a managerial position are no longer power and authority. Eighty-nine percent of employees want to be a manager if they can share their knowledge and experience with others. Eighty-five percent find it attractive to be responsible for the success of an organization; being able to influence decisions is another positive. These elements, unsurprisingly, are the oft-cited benefits of having an empowered workforce versus a command-and-control workplace.[46]

In the first chapter, we reviewed the burning platform and why the decade of 2010 is the perfect time for EPowerment. We have also discussed at length two of the three Es that comprise EPowerment: the e world and emotional intelligence.

In this chapter, we explore empowerment in more detail. After this chapter, we anticipate you will be saying, "Okay, I got it. Now how do I make it happen?" We will present an overview of the five essential learning principles to get to EPowerment personally, professionally, and organizationally and create that sought-after state of empowerment. And in each of the successive chapters, one of the five principles will be explored in greater detail.

Empowerment: The Unrealized Promise

Discussed in part in chapter 1, empowerment is worth more elaboration to establish the context for the five learning principles.

> *Engaging employees will be another critical ability leaders of the future must possess. That one requires mutual ownership over everything.*
>
> —Ruth Kennedy, director of organization development, VF Corporation

The practice of empowerment was established in the early '90s. In the pursuit of quality and efficiency, we discovered that decision making was located too high in the hierarchy. The people who had the authority to make decisions lacked the knowledge necessary to make good decisions because they were too far removed from the details of work processes involved in getting the work done. Those closest to the work know what is affecting the quality of their work but lack the authority to make decisions to get their work done while hitting the mark regarding standards of quality. Empowerment meant authorizing decision-making responsibility to those who were as close to the work and the customer as possible.

Efforts to delegate authority took a variety of forms, from quality circles to self-directed work teams. The underlying principle focused on allowing the people most intimately involved in the details of the work to make decisions when they needed to be made. Every effort was made to eliminate needless hierarchical barriers to decision-making.

> *People at our stores know how to drive sales. All we have to do is ask them. We put so much restraint on people. If you are able to unleash people, you can*

*create amazing things. Too often we don't ask and
when we do ask, it is even more rare that we listen.*

—Susan Richter, director of human resources,
Food Lion, LLC

Starting with Deming's work in the 1980s, employee participation and empowerment became the watchword for those interested in leadership and organizational development.[47] A steady stream of leadership gurus proclaimed that we were on the verge of organizational transformation in a never-ending pursuit of quality. Books were written. Speeches proclaimed a new age. Organizations embarked in massive efforts to restructure themselves and their leadership.

Granted, many companies have shown notable results by creating employee participation and involvement in decision making. In theory, empowerment of the workforce makes sense. But, as history shows, the promise of empowerment failed to live up to our hopes.

*I believe a leader is someone who creates a compelling
vision of the future and mobilizes people to achieve
that vision.*

—-Randy Brown, chief human resources
officer, WellPoint

The initial principles of empowerment were simple and based on common sense:

- Empowerment means that decision making is distributed throughout the organization rather than relying solely on traditional top-down authority.
- Significant savings and efficiencies are available by accumulating even small incremental changes.

- Employees shall either make decisions or offer opinions before decisions are made that directly affect their work.
- Employees are assumed to be comfortable enough to drive or influence decision making.
- Managers will be personally inclined and interpersonally adept at encouraging participation through listening and delegating authority appropriately.
- Managers and employees are expected to understand the necessity of empowerment and embrace the changes in organizational structure and relationships necessary to make it happen.
- We assume that everyone values and will pursue the personal growth available in a participatory culture.
- Finally, we assume that everyone will have the knowledge and skill sets necessary to participate appropriately in decision making. Where knowledge is lacking, training is expected to close the gaps.

On the face of it, the argument for empowerment is so compelling that you'd think we'd have transformed the way we get things done in the workplace by now. Sadly, real-life business results fall far short of the ideal.

> *Many HR initiatives fail because people don't seek input from those working close to the change. In my team, all new processes go through a cross-functional team, which leads to better decision making and more support for the change.*
> —Bob Zierk, VP of human resources at Black & Decker

While progress has been made, why do we have so far to go?

In addition to the reasons previously discussed, a few additional short answers will suffice. Discontinuous change takes time and sustained attention. People do not always have the time or the information to act, even if they are empowered to do so. Empowerment all too often fails due to the lack of the consistent leadership support that is necessary to make it happen. Finally, people on the front lines may lack the skill sets, resourcefulness, and the personal and organizational connectivity necessary to sustain empowerment over the long term. Essentially, empowerment has failed because the other two E's (leveraging the e world and EQ) are not being integrated.

> *It is imperative to make training available to all people in the organization. A focus on salaried employees will help the bottom line. When you invest time and money in the leaders of the organization, they will be empowered to be effective leaders and that multiplies impact across the organization. Every employee deserves to be the best. Try to reach as many people as possible and provide as many development opportunities as possible.*
>
> —Linda Worden, director of training & organizational development, MeadWestvaco Corporation

EPOWERMENT

Leader: Todd Harrison, director of leadership and associate development, WellPoint, Inc.

Todd Harrison designed and implemented a robust talent management strategy for all 42,000 managers and employees across the company that fosters a culture where career development is associate-owned and manager-supported. He ensures that the development of leaders and associates results in them being capable of driving change and transforming the organization.

Company:
WellPoint, Inc. operates in the health insurance industry. The company has primarily domestic operations in fourteen states as the licensee of Blue Cross and Blue Shield Products and offers additional health benefits services such as dental, vision, life, and non-Blue health products across the United States. WellPoint's subsidiaries include Anthem Blue Cross and Empire Blue Cross Blue Shield. Annual revenue is $60 billion with 42,000 employees supporting its mission. WellPoint's Promise Statement is, "We will simplify the connection between health, care, and value."

Point of View:
The essence of leadership is to create an atmosphere that gets others to want to do what we are convinced must be done.

- *On Empowerment*: I believe you should hire people, put them in the right position, provide them with the vision and the proper resources at their point-of-need, and then turn away—supporting them, if needed.
- *On Extended Learning*: Take the initiative to make things better by working to continuously improve yourself, the environment in which you work, and those around you.
- *On Emotional Safety*: Everyone should challenge the norms. It is important to constantly search for new and better ways of doing things. Do not be afraid to make a change when needed, and never be satisfied with the status quo. I tell my employees, "Be candid and forthright in your dealings with me. Tell me what I need to hear, not what you think I want to hear."

EPOWERMENT

- *On Courage*: The only unforgivable mistake is to do nothing when a decision is required. Do something, even if it turns out to be wrong.
- *On Teamwork*: It is the responsibility of everyone to create a motivating environment. Teams must recognize the contributions of each member and take time to celebrate our accomplishments.

Best Practices:
WellPoint has undergone a shift in mindset regarding talent development. Following a long history of a paternalistic approach to career development, we are now implementing a system that is owned and driven by employees. In order to accomplish the level of transformational change, we did the following:

1. Created and consistently communicated a motivating change story.
2. Developed an orderly, sequenced portfolio of initiatives for reaching goals.
3. Aligned our top team around what they need to do to lead the organization.
4. Built the leadership capacity to drive change and initiate success.
5. Actively aligned the culture to support our mission and promise.
6. Built energy throughout the organization through a combination of symbolic actions and by engaging the front line.
7. Created a process for tracking our performance.

Every activity, event, or exercise presents a learning opportunity. Take time to evaluate what you are doing, individually and organizationally, and share your lessons learned with others. Think about learning on three levels—self, team, and organization. Ensure learning and development opportunities are meaningful and realistic and tied to the business.

The Five Principles for Achieving EPowerment

Effective personal and professional development is, and always will be, the result of learning. However, the old ways of learning are no longer relevant in a knowledge economy in the e world. Exposure to information is not enough to ensure learning. Most of us forget what we read in textbooks; even if we do remember, the information will be outdated a few years after publication. We have already talked about the impact of technology making the half-life of knowledge shorter and shorter. Attending an event, such as management training, does not produce lasting changes in behavior on the job.

Learning must be experiential and dynamic. For maximum benefit, processing experiences must occur shortly after they occur and when the learner is ready to process them. Thus, a new, unique solution for personal and professional development is needed.

> *At WellPoint, we are moving from a paternalistic, hand-holding style (e.g., "this is your training and this is your next career move.") to an employee-driven model. Career progression is not necessarily vertical. Career accountability is on the employees themselves, whether that means expanded responsibility in the current role, moving up, moving down, or making a lateral move. The focus is on the employee, while the manager provides support and resources.*
>
> —Todd Harrison, director of leadership and associate development, WellPoint

We are proud to present a new model to achieve EPowerment. We argue that the five principles in the new model will allow for powerful and unprecedented states of empowerment, high levels of EQ, and maximizing the e world. The dichotomy, discussed earlier, between our personal lives and our professional lives can be eliminated by mandating that these five principles collectively be integrated into our organizations.

The five learning principles are:

1. Extended learning models: Make learning a process, not an event.

2. Emotional safety: Make it safe to say "I don't know," "I need help," or "That's a bad idea."

3. Mentoring: The timeless model of passing wisdom that only comes from those traveling in front of us.

4. Multi-mode learning: One size does not fit all. Give folks what they need, at the time they need it, and in the manner they can best receive it to make better decisions.

5. Outcome-based learning: If learning cannot be correlated to a desired high-performance metric, eliminate it.

We will explore each of these principles in great detail. As we do, consider our definition of the perfect learning experience: no matter who you are, no matter where you are, and no matter what your need, if at the time you require it, you can access knowledge—irrespective of the source—to help you make a better decision, then that is the perfect learning experience; that is empowerment.

EPowerment captures the elusive "how to" of empowerment. By leveraging technologies to connect in real time and focusing on EQ as experiences occur, empowerment can finally be truly achieved. Empowerment has a tremendous personal impact. By using the e world to provide easy access to information and worldwide instantaneous communication, the stage is set for a new generation of knowledge workers ready for empowerment.

Summary and Key Points

- The original concept of empowerment touted giving decision-making power to the front lines.
- The implementation of empowerment fell short of the ideal vision.
- Empowerment failed because we lacked the proper tools and the appropriate culture to do it right.
- Today, people and organizations have changed. Leaders no longer seek power and organizations no longer chase accountability.
- Five principles can make empowerment achievable. EPowerment is a new model that captures the missing piece of empowerment.
- The five principles of EPowerment are extended learning models, emotional safety, mentoring, multimode learning, and outcome-based learning.

Chapter 5
The Extended Learning Model

The Japanese word "kaizen" means "improvement." In Japan, it is common to label industrial or business improvement techniques with the word kaizen, and thus, the word kaizen has evolved, in the English language, to be synonymous with the implementation of continuous improvement.

Kaizen is a daily activity, going above and beyond simple productivity improvement. It is also a process that humanizes the workplace while eliminating overly hard work and boosting profits. Employees are empowered to perform experiments on their work using the scientific method, which allows them to spot and eliminate waste in business processes. Win, win, win.

As we finalize our transition from an industrial economy to the knowledge economy, how can we use kaizen to empower people? Our focus needs to not be on the automated process improvement that we relied on for profits in years past and, instead, needs to include thoughtful, creative, strategic tactics that the knowledge age requires. What would happen if, instead of conducting experiments on their work, people conducted experiments on themselves, foundationally improving the core of what makes them perform? "Kaizen, the Japanese philosophy of continuous development, is embedded in our culture at Fidelity," says Bill Hodgetts, VP of corporate leadership development at Fidelity.

To bring kaizen into professional learning and development, a major shift in the concept of learning needs to happen. Over the past thirty-plus years, we have experienced event-based learning models comprising conferences, seminars, workshops, speakers, and newer versions of events including Webinars.

These old ways of *learning* have paralleled the old ways of *doing*. Without technology, students of all types gathered in a room and listened to an "expert." Whether that expert was a teacher, a professor, a consultant, a researcher, or the boss, the process of an event-based learning model was the same. But unfortunately, the outcome was the same, too.

The Limitations of Event-based Learning

Event-based learning didn't work yesterday, it doesn't work today, and it will not work tomorrow, whether it is enabled by technological innovations or not. Sending people off to a day or two of training is unlikely to meet the EPowerment criteria or result in effective and substantive learning. This is because event-based training has a honeymoon period where there is an excitement reaction in response to being exposed to a new idea. What follows is a steep drop-off in the retention of knowledge. Knowledge is lost soon after the seminar, class, or reading is completed.

Knowledge is soon lost for several reasons, and all those reasons have to do with the fact that events are constricted in time, spanning a few contiguous days, a few hours, or a few minutes. This is a problem.

1. *Events are scheduled.* But the readiness for learning is impossible to predetermine. On the day of the training, there is little likelihood that people will be ready and motivated to engage in learning. How does a leader select those who will be ready to learn on a specific date and time?

2. *Emotions are transient.* Individuals are in different emotional and motivational states when they get back to work than they were when they experienced the training. Going back to work seems like a journey back to reality rather than an event marked by excitement about applying newly acquired competencies.

3. *The mode of learning does not appeal to all learners.* Event-based events tend to rely on lectures, discussions, and, perhaps, the learning and practice of new skills. Any given event will be attended by people who have different learning styles and who access information in different ways. The methodology brought to the design of a given event will appeal to some people but not to others.

4. *Connecting the dots is difficult.* Once a workshop is completed and people go back to work, there is little to support them in the integration of conceptual learning and the application of new behaviors and competencies on the job.

Scheduled learning events are based on the flawed assumption that the learner will be ready to learn the material presented, ready to learn in the modality designed, and ready to apply what was just learned. As we all know, the likelihood that these three elements will all spontaneously occur at a pre-determined date and time is almost none.

In the EPowerment world, barriers must be eliminated for the learner. EPowered working professionals should have access to learning from wherever they are and whenever they need it, so that they can apply it instantly. This is the only way to convert those learning moments, which are highly unpredictable, to those *aha!* moments that signal substantive learning that is more likely to be applied back on the job. *Instant* and *point-of-need* based learning is a characteristic of EPowerment. The probability of capturing more learning moments and converting more of them into *aha!* moments increases dramatically in extended learning models. This can only happen by leveraging technologies that allow for learning that parallels real life and real needs.

The challenge of producing real learning over the course of a single presentation has increasingly haunted development professionals. Ken Blanchard, a noted author and leadership guru, is reported to have started a presentation in the following way: "Only one of you in this group will actually take what we cover today and put it to use on the job. The rest of you are here to make sure that person's learning is cost-effective."

Recent research has underscored the limitations of event-based learning. In spite of all the hard work put into developing materials and the mastery of platform skills by so many professional trainers, attendance in a single training event is unlikely to produce significant improvement. A collection of training research finds that only 10 percent of all training results in any transfer of knowledge beyond the training room. Approximately 40 percent of content is transferred immediately following training. Unfortunately, the amount retained falls to 25 percent after six months and 15 percent after one year.[48]

Event-based learning is fundamentally flawed because its approach is in opposition to our learning style. Information learned over a period of time is retained better and longer than information learned in one sitting. This is due to the spacing effect of learning, which has been found over and over in research studies worldwide—actually the research goes back to the 1920s.[49] Brain cells are generated over time and putting them to use enhances their survival. But the important distinction is that learning enhances cell survival—not simply exposure to training. Learning over an extended period of time induces a more persistent memory.[50]

> *Curriculum by itself doesn't provide depth and breadth—you must include self-initiated learning that is self-paced and tied to your needs. So learning must be business-objective oriented and calibrated to the individual. Include three components: 1) timely, 2) flexible, and 3) bite-sized. It is a dynamic world, however, and by the time you have designed a curriculum, it is already outdated.*
>
> —Effenus Henderson, chief diversity officer, Weyerhaeuser

Event-based learning isn't totally worthless; it is good for building awareness. It is great for the first time you are exposed to a concept, a theory, or a new way of looking at either yourself or the world. Events are effective and appropriate for learning one message or one skill that does, indeed, fit all, such as learning a company-wide policy or building awareness about a safety initiative.

But event-based learning falls short when we want substantive learning—that learning that sticks with employees, that learning resulting from an *aha!* moment. Substantive learning requires that several essentials intersect with the learning experience for retention of adequate knowledge. The odds of success improve when individuals learn over an extended period of time, such as six months or a year. In an extended learning model, the constraints of timing diminished because we are learning as we go—as our needs change from moment to moment.

> *The greatest, fastest, and most impressive change I have ever seen was after a reflective experience or in response to feedback that created awareness. Until people gather their own data and see a disconnect between where they are now, and where they could be—until that click occurs, the best learning tools and workshops will not produce behavioral change.*
>
> —Troy Heflin, VP of organizational development, Volvo

Consider *aha!* moments again—those flashes of insight that occur when we suddenly see an aspect of our experience and ourselves in new ways. *Aha!* moments are unpredictable and cannot be orchestrated. They are most likely to occur when the timing of readiness, modality, and application come together. This is why American Society for Training and Development (ASTD) industry reports repeatedly show that over 70 percent of workplace learning occurs informally. We call this *point-of-need learning.* When you learn at the point-of-need—that can only occur in an extended model—the odds, again, of having many *aha!* moments go up significantly.

The problem with many training programs is that they are not relevant to participants' jobs. Therefore the participants' motivation to learn is not being tapped. Employees may act as if they care about learning something and go through the motions, but in the end they will disregard it or forget it—unless it is something they want or need to learn. While much of corporate America is involved actively in training, much of that training fails to be germane to any individual's job. [51] Instead, it falls short, is too comprehensive, is inappropriate, is geared to the wrong audience, or it doesn't follow sound training principles. "It seems easy to get so caught up in training people around new fads, processes, and procedures, new business technologies and techniques, and all the bells and whistles," a director of training and development for a Fortune 500 company says. "It seems that we are in such a rush that we fail to train people to perform their actual job effectively."

> *At WellPoint, we are moving toward a strategy that focuses on taking the learning to the worker versus the traditional way of taking the worker to the learning. This is, in essence, an example of the point-of-need approach. We have seen this borne out in the way we have seen our associates use our e-learning courses. The percentage of associates who registered for our online courses versus those who completed the courses was horribly low; just around 14 percent of those who registered actually completed the e-learning courses. As we began to diagnose the issue, we began to see a theme emerge from*

our surveys and focus groups in that the majority of the associates were going into a course, finding the information they needed, and then logging out. They had figured out how to create a point-of-need resource for themselves out of a traditional online course. This led us to the implementation of a new tool that provides one-click access to content on more than 500 topics in an online Flash video format lasting three to five minutes. Our utilization rate of this new tool is around 45 percent of our associate audience (roughly 20,000 associates) each year for the past two years.

—Todd Harrison, director of leadership and associate development, WellPoint

Ineffective training wastes precious resources. Past research[52] has shown that managers cited poor training as the cause for quality problems, internal and external customer dissatisfaction, poor morale and bad attitudes among employees, and lost teamwork and cooperation. But yet, they also said that no training at all has the same effect. Additional costs to companies include misuse of systems and equipment, increased turnover and absenteeism, safety compliance problems, and difficulty in meeting goals.

Let us also not forget the cost factor. Event-based models are costly (tuition, travel, expenses, time off) in contrast to leveraging the technologies discussed in chapter 2 that are already being used in our personal lives.

EXTENDED LEARNING MODEL

Leader: Linda Worden, director of training & organizational development, MeadWestvaco Corporation

Linda oversees training activities, organization development, leadership development, and coaching for the senior employees of the consumer and office products division.

Company:
MeadWestvaco Corporation (MWV) has annual revenues of $7 billion and employs more than 20,000 people worldwide. MWV is a global packaging company that provides packaging solutions to many of the world's premiere brands in the healthcare, personal and beauty care, food, beverage, tobacco, media and entertainment, and home and garden industries. MWV's other business segments include consumer and office products, specialty chemicals, and land management.

Point of View:
The mission of a human resources department is to provide the right people to the organization in order to accomplish strategic objectives. It is imperative to make critical strategic training available to all people in the organization. A focus on salaried employees will help the bottom line. When you invest time and money in the leaders of the organization, they will be empowered to be effective leaders, and that multiplies impact across the organization. Every employee deserves to be the best. Try to reach as many people as possible and provide as many development opportunities as possible.

Best Practices:
There is a need for people to understand the value of the extended learning model. Too many people have the mental model that learning is "that one-day training event that I go to." We have an opportunity to get people to understand the extended learning model. Our strategy this year is "training is an event, learning is a process."

EXTENDED LEARNING MODEL

MWV's leadership development program is built on the extended learning model, from line leader training to pre-work e-learning. Learners come together for one week, work on case studies, take a three-month break, and then reinforce their learning with another week of training. Following that, there's another three-month break before another week-long training session. We make sure to do a pre- and post assessment.

Everyone is an expert at something and can share his or her experience, knowledge, and wisdom with others. Some best practices for sharing knowledge freely are:

- Clarify the needs by getting people in the mode of thinking about problems and gaps daily.
- Encourage employees to identify learning opportunities.
- Think about new ways of learning as opposed to training.
- Break training needs into smaller pieces.

The Failure of Diversity Training

In chapter 1, we discussed diversity in the context of globalization. To review, our newfound access to so many people from so many different backgrounds can be a powerful EPowerment tool, if leveraged correctly.

In recent years, diversity training has become a staple for many organizations. The intentions behind this training are honorable. Diversity training is designed to help people become more aware of their prejudices and to be more open to diverse points of view brought into the workplace by people with varying gender, racial, ethnic, and national backgrounds.

In spite of the resources still being poured into diversity training, a recent study[53] of diversity programs found that their impact is minimal. The study reported a comprehensive review of thirty-one years of data from 830 mid-size to large U.S. workplaces. It found that the kind of diversity training exercises offered at most firms were followed by a 7.5 percent *drop* in the number of women in management. The number of black, female managers fell by 10 percent, and the number of black men in top positions fell by 12 percent. Similar effects were seen for Latinos and Asians.

The study concluded that mandatory programs—often undertaken mainly with an eye to avoiding liability in discrimination lawsuits—were the problem. When diversity training is voluntary and undertaken to advance a company's business goals, it was associated with increased diversity in management. "The [training sessions aren't working because they] are more symbolic than substantive," said Lauren Edelman, a University of California professor of law and sociology, who independently reviewed the study.

Learning Moments
Dr. Izzy Justice

I can't tell you how many times I have said to myself, "Every day I have a chance to learn something new and from at least one person I come in contact with." I mean just take inventory of your day yesterday—how many people did you talk to on the phone, how many e-mails and text messages did you craft or respond to, how many meetings (in person or virtually) did you attend? At the end of each day or week or month, I rarely ask myself: What did I learn today? Who did I learn it from? How am I using this "lesson" to make myself, others, or my business better?

I confuse reading an inspiring quote with learning. I confuse a really productive conversation with learning. I confuse reading a good book with learning. But what is learning if there is no thought of incorporating that new knowledge into your behavior, skills, and daily actions to make yourself, others, and your business better? If you're not learning *and* making subsequent changes, then you're regressing. I have a good friend who played professional football in the NFL who says, "If we're not on offense, someone else is trying to score on us." If we're not *proactively* converting our learnings to make changes, no matter how trivial many of them may be, then the learnings are for naught.

Think of the experiences you have each day that can produce personal growth by simply exploring life in this curious manner. The personal growth you will experience will be dramatic compared to those who choose to do what most of us do— enduring challenges and moving on to the next ones without considering what they can learn from them.

Memory as the Enemy of Learning

Corporate development has much to learn from recent advances in training for health-care professionals.

Information recall, like multiple-choice tests, is the lowest format of training. The problem is the world is an open-book exam.

—VP of training and development at a major retail chain

Memory-based care has been the *modus operandi* for clinicians throughout the world for centuries. The delivery of treatment occurs on the spot, based on what the clinician knows and remembers from his or her medical training. There is a problem though: medical errors are a major cause of death in the United States. Bad physicians do not cause these errors. Good physicians make mistakes because, at the point of care, they lack access to all the latest and pertinent information regarding the patient and potential treatment options.

A study published over ten years ago in the Institute of Medicine showed that there are over 100,000 deaths per year in the United States (conservatively) that occur due to medical errors.[54] Again, it is worth noting that these errors are not committed by bad clinicians; these errors are committed because, at the time that the treatment was prescribed in the examination room, there was not enough data to alert the clinician of relevant issues.

For example, the doctor knows that, given a certain set of symptoms, the appropriate prescription is 200 mg of drug X. The doctor—at that moment—may be unaware of a recent study showing that the dosage of that drug prescribed for this patient had certain side effects previously unknown. The doctor may also not be aware of other drugs the patient may be taking that might produce adverse reactions. Clearly there is a great deal of information and data points that a clinician has to store, recollect, and retrieve from memory all at the right time and all in a matter of seconds. As a consequence, medical errors contribute to the third-most-prevalent cause of death in the United States.

There is a growing trend to convert medicine and health care from a memory-based care to a knowledge-driven care model that integrates memory and best practices in a way that makes information available to the clinician at the point of care. In this revised model, the physician will have access to data on the patient and be able to draw on external sources of clinical knowledge and practices at the point of care. This will lead to better patient care than that provided by physicians who rely solely on memory in determining what course to take in treating a given patient.

Why should this rationale not apply to *all* professionals? Why should any working professionals rely on memory to make the best decisions for themselves and the companies they work for? Physicians need access to clinical history and information regarding potential courses of treatment. Other professionals also need access to best practices, case studies, articles, etc., so that at the time that they need information, they can access it and make better decisions.

With as much data as we have flying at us in this new millennium (e-mails, calls, appointments, text messaging, etc.), our memory is not the best place to store and retrieve valuable information, especially in health care, where the consequences can be fatal. The shift to "knowledge-driven care" provides best practices, patient profiles, and other data to clinicians at the point of care so that unintentional poor decisions are minimized or eliminated entirely. In other words, complementing memory with knowledge at the point of care is the secret recipe. This is a characteristic of EPowerment and only possible by leveraging technology and having high levels of EQ.

> *I was recently taking the GRE for admission into a doctoral program. The GRE, like all other standardized tests, requires the person taking the test to rely predominantly on memory or IQ to answer the questions. During the exam I came upon a word I had never read before and therefore was not able to answer the question without guessing. Immediately after I completed the exam, I promptly Googled the word to find out its meaning. In doing so, I was struck by how our old forms of "testing" based on the memory model are quickly becoming antiquated and should be replaced with a more relevant, knowledge-based model.*
>
> —Todd Harrison, director of leadership and associate development, WellPoint

How is this relevant to those of us not in health care but in management or leadership roles? Though the consequences of our bad decisions may not be fatal, dramatic, or immediate, we too are relying on our memories and experiences to make daily decisions. In the workplace, we often make decisions where consequences show up way down the line, sometimes in someone else's business processes and departments, and when the poor decisions are identified for discussion, we often raise our hands, point somewhere else and say, "Well, I did not have all the right data."

Working professionals, especially managers and leaders,

need to avoid relying solely on memory. Instead, we should be complementing our memories with knowledge at the time when decisions are being made. With easy access to technology, this has never been more doable and it is relatively easy to systemize across organizations. Organizations that provide this knowledge at the *point-of-need* for their managers and leaders will clearly avoid more mistakes than those that don't. And for those of us in the consulting, training, development, and coaching world, consider this: if what we teach our clients is predicated on them remembering what we teach them, then we are falling far short of empowering our clients.

Our memory is not like a hard drive on a computer where once an item is stored, it can be searched for and retrieved in the same manner it was stored. Our memory, which most of us use either predominantly or exclusively to make decisions every day at work, is a tool that is clearly susceptible to emotion—it is unreliable, transient, and inaccurate. This is where EQ comes into play.

It is truly a shame that the academic system rewards those with better memories. In a world where we now have truly unprecedented channels that can reliably connect and access people, communities, and knowledge sources, the primary tool for good decision making should not be memory. Instead, the primary tools should be versatility and resourcefulness to adapt and connect from anywhere and at anytime. We are convinced that the most successful of working professionals in the new decade will be those who have this versatility and resourcefulness, those who are EPowered. In contrast, those of us stuck in the ways we were brought up, from a learning perspective, will become increasingly irrelevant.

Personal Growth Tip: Draw a Line

Draw a line somewhere toward the bottom of your calendar, to-do list, or daily agenda, and leave a space for one or two bullet points. Write down in fewer than five words what you learn each day. At the end of the week, look at them and choose one item to incorporate and practice the following week. Learn to learn, learn to change, learn every day.

Extended learning models, as opposed to event-based learning models, provide a much larger window of opportunity to grow, both personally and professionally. Every learning experience your organization offers should consider learning moments of their employees—when they occur, how they occur, where they occur. Then, based on this, extended learning models can be created. This will allow employees the greatest opportunity to convert as many of these learning moments to *aha!* moments. Capture the *aha!* moments and you can correlate the number of them to your success. As more conversions are accumulated, better decisions will be made and consequently, the performance of the individual and the organization will improve.

As a leader, attempt to proactively transform your environment—even if it's just for the moment or just for the day. Consider starting every meeting by asking those in the meeting what their learning moments were the previous week and how many of them were converted to *aha!* moments. Employees might learn and begin copying improved methods from one another. These positive experiences will pile up and be a great source of strength, credibility, and success tomorrow and in the future.

At the macro level, the corporate learning and development philosophy at Coca-Cola Bottling is that we fundamentally believe that we have to increase our capability as a learning organization. That means creating a culture of innovation and appropriate and thoughtful risk-taking. Embedded in that is a requirement that HR systems are aligned with that objective. The way employees are rewarded, recognized, and admonished is aligned with our culture of innovation and thoughtful risk-taking. On an individual level, the number one required skill is intellectual curiosity—we encourage and expect people to be curious about things, ask questions, and challenge the status quo. Poke and prod at the "why" in front of the "what," the "how," and the "who." The goal is to build that capability now, so that over time we become an active learning environment where learning isn't an activity that happens methodically but is embedded in who we are and what we do.

—Kevin Henry, chief HR officer, Coca-Cola
Bottling Consolidated Co.

Rather than limiting learning to event-based training programs, we learn best if we engage in a learning experience when events in our lives and work indicate a need for improved skills and knowledge. This is great news. After grappling with the mediocre results of traditional event-based training programs, we can now truly help people learn by creating and implementing extended learning experiences. With immediate access to any book, any article, and any other person that technology provides, we can now all be experts.

Summary and Key Points

- Event-based learning models are not the ideal way to learn.
- Event-based learning is scheduled ahead of time, but readiness to learn cannot be predetermined.
- Our emotions are transient—we need to apply new knowledge when we are passionate about it.
- Events are great when we want to learn from an expert.
- Learning cannot be commanded, prescribed, or authorized. It happens slowly, naturally, and over time as a result of experiences.
- If you want someone to learn something, events are too expensive and too inefficient to be relied on.
- Diversity appreciation is not a result of training; it is a result of understanding.
- For high performance, relying on memory is not scalable in an information-overloaded world.
- Memory-based performance can now be supplemented by instant access to information and knowledge at the point of need.
- Performance is moving from a memory-based model to a knowledge-based model.

Chapter 6
Emotional Safety

Walter Chrysler has said, "Whenever there is a hard job to be done, I assign it to a lazy man; he is sure to find an easy way of doing it."

This perspective presents an open-minded, compassionate way of looking at your employees. Many authoritarian bosses might simply fire the one who appears to not be working. But alas, that lazy employee may be the most authentic, the most productive, and in turn—one of the most valuable members of your team. This is because these employees don't accept work as it is presented to them; they have the courage to strive to find the best and easiest way to get it done. Thinking about the changes our world will face in the upcoming decade, the lazy man will have the upper hand in creating and innovating the way operations are run. The work that can be done as is without any tweaks, shortcuts, or improvements is the work that will be outsourced. But the ability to question the status quo, the guts to ignore your manager's request and do it your way, and the mental agility to even entertain that option, first requires an EPowered individual who feels emotionally safe in the organization.[55]

Most of us have little to fear regarding our physical safety at work. We are not afraid when we walk into a building that the building might fall on us or that we will get robbed in the elevator. Physical safety, often an unspoken expectation, is critical for people to show up at work. When you ask an organization what they do to make sure their employees are safe, the list of security interventions is long, as it should be. But ask the same employers what they do for the emotional safety of their employees, and you will likely get a blank stare. In fact, as of this writing, if you Google "emotional safety" or even "emotional safety at work", you will get millions of results, but none that are directly applicable to working professionals.

Yet, emotional safety is essential in an environment that encourages participation in decision-making and continuous learning, in creating a truly empowered culture. Without emotional safety, we become paralyzed, and empowerment is not possible. Unfortunately, the workplace has a number of factors that can combine to threaten the emotional safety of people each and every day. And, since 38 percent of us work more than forty-four hours a week, this is no small matter, undoubtedly spilling over to our home lives and well-being.[56]

Hierarchy

Currently, the structure of the overwhelming majority of organizations is such that relationships at work are defined by differences in power and authority. Some managers are adept at handling authority, while others have a tendency to be authoritarian and punitive in dealing with their direct reports. It has been said that people don't leave their work, they leave their managers. But it's not a problem with the managers necessarily; it's a problem with the system. If you give one entity a paternalistic role, the other one naturally takes a dependent role. When there is hierarchy, responsibility and accountability are not shared equally, making empowerment literally impossible, as the people lower in the corporate structure must look up to those with authority for every decision and action. Even the best managers will struggle, at first, to find a way to overcome the system. We are not making it easy to have good relationships, and the quality of the relationships between people and their bosses has a huge impact on the experience of emotional safety, or the lack of it.

> *Ideally, you want a flat organization. The more we have hierarchy, the faster the younger generation slips out of our hands.*
>
> —Anne Feller, Cox Communications

If you're going to use hierarchy, use it for good. Steve Larson, who is senior VP of diversity, engagement, and inclusion at Wells Fargo, recommends that if you want change to happen, you should use a top-down strategy. Build awareness for the senior leaders first. Allow for intensive awareness experiences. That education will then cascade down. Leaders will create similar experiences for their team and they will be able to provide coaching support once they themselves learn how.

Personal History

From early in life, people develop a pattern for their relationship to authority that is then played out in their working lives. Some people develop a fear of people in authority, which makes emotional safety unavailable to them whenever they are faced with such a situation. Similarly, personal history can define the associations we have developed with risk-taking, expanding our comfort zones, or establishing new relationships. While this is by no means a permanent state, if patterns are not recognized, the situation will not improve.

How Can Leaders Encourage Risk-Taking in People Whose Life Experiences Leave Them Risk-Averse?

Anger avoidance and conflict avoidance come from lack of skill in managing chaos and uncertainty and negative expectations of the outcome. The goal is to shift the mindset from a defensive place to one where there is openness and comfort with conflict and conflict is something that can be viewed as a learning experience. To accomplish that:

1. Set boundaries.

2. Create a safe space and a supportive environment.

3. Give opportunities to experiment with new or intimidating situations.

4. Show that constructive conflict is okay and can be positive.

5. Teach competencies such as assertiveness skills and active listening.

*Tips from Steve Larson of Wells Fargo and Letitia Knowles of American Express shared during the HR professionals Webinar on emotional safety.

Personality Differences

Personal conflicts can reduce emotional safety. Very often, the root cause of such interpersonal conflicts is witnessing behavior we do not understand or experiencing an interaction that confuses us. We each have a unique, innate style that is molded by our life experiences, and the multiple ways that it is manifested can cause tension. The tension comes from a lack of empathy, a finalized or inflexible mind map of the world, or a belief system that "my way is the right way." When people do not easily get along with their managers or some of their coworkers, it is difficult for them to feel at ease or be willing to take the risks necessary for growth and learning.

EMOTIONAL SAFETY

Leader: Jane Luciano, vice president of global learning and organization development, Bristol-Myers Squibb

Company:
Bristol-Myers Squibb is a global biopharmaceutical company dedicated to helping patients prevail against serious disease.

Point of View:
The group I lead is an internal organizational development team. In reality, we provide services that can easily be bought externally. The value proposition is that we can do it cheaper, faster, better—our deep knowledge of the organization and continuity help with this, but we must also stay on our learning edge. Having "one foot inside the company and one foot outside of the company" gives objectivity to our work.

Best Practices:
Leaders must risk being vulnerable by sharing ideas, successes, and failures to create space for different ideas, opinions, and exchanges. To make a good decision, you have to have the courage to say "no" in front of a whole room of people saying "yes;" you must have the courage to voice a point of view that is the opposite and the courage to ask, "Have you thought of this?" To help decision making at the collective level so we don't hear from the same three voices talk all the time, we use methods like private collection and seeking disconfirming data to hear more of the breadth and magnitude of ideas. The results are innovation that creates value, increased speed in decision making, and the start of a learning organization.

EMOTIONAL SAFETY

In all our change work, we talk about creating a safe place. At the start of any change initiative, most people feel good about their performance and capability. Through the change, we ask employees to go down on performance for some period of time so they have capacity to learn new skills—increase their capability. This acknowledgement and expectation of a dip in performance creates that safe environment for people to do that learning. We know that, ultimately, performance and capability will go up after they learn (or unlearn—sometimes you have to let go of what you are comfortable with). This is how a safe environment is built into every change plan.

As an example, we recently moved e-mail systems. That caused a capability dip across the board for a short period of time. Whether people took the training or not beforehand, their capability dropped temporarily. But it was important to focus on the longer-term, bigger picture outcome—we are on one system globally now. Our partners have the same system, which has resulted in better collaboration and new capabilities. The new system now has better benefits than the old one did, but it took a dip in performance to get there. A saying I have that illustrates this concept well is, "Leaders need to help people see that staying still is less safe than learning in this fast-paced world of change."

Stages of change:

1. Awareness: I heard of it
2. Understanding: I get it

> *The gap between "I get it" and "I live it" is huge because it means I have to change my behavior.*

3. Buy-in: I live it*
4. Ownership: I sponsor it

*Everyone has to get to "I live it."

Value Differences

Similar to personality differences, significant value differences between coworkers or with managers can leave people feeling ill at ease. Interpretation of values is a thin line that gets crossed every day, creating room for constant doubt and need for self-preservation. The interesting twist in this isn't necessarily overtly expressed value differences, but the values we assume others carry based on the behaviors they exhibit. When value differences exist, managers must ensure that the environment allows for the ability to understand and get along. Sometimes our working environments create barriers to inclusiveness. A supportive environment must include accountability, but it must also have a sense of humanity.

> *People are afraid to step outside of their comfort zone and appreciate differences. Instead, fear drives their interactions, and that limits their power and effectiveness. Help people overcome fear. Don't characterize individuals; that takes attention off of the real issues. Seek to understand different perspectives. Valuing individual differences requires a lifelong learner approach. Help people be more inclusive through encouraging learning, growth, and development. Those that don't value differences will have an impediment.*
>
> —Effenus Henderson, chief diversity officer, Weyerhaeuser

Diversity

The workplace is already changing, and the change is sure to accelerate in the future. Change, even positive change, can produce what appear to be personal threats that affect perceptions of emotional safety. The workforce is increasingly diverse in terms of race, ethnicity, differences in generational values and orientation to work, and gender issues. From 2010 to 2030, the U.S. Census Bureau projects that the proportion of the U.S. population in each of several minority groups will rise: African Americans, from 12.9 percent to 13.3 percent; Asians, from 5.1 percent to 7.1 percent; and Hispanics, from 16.0 percent to 23 percent. At the same time, the proportion of white, non-Hispanic U.S. residents will decrease from 66.1 percent to 57.5 percent.

The core of the problem is that we are naturally biased. Just as we're better at recognizing people who share our ethnicity, we are also better at interpreting the emotional facial expressions of people from the same ethnic, national, or regional group as ourselves. In an experiment, sixty participants were instructed to interpret the facial expressions of men who were randomly labeled as either basketball players or non-players. For half the participants, the labels were switched to be sure the crucial factor was how the faces were labeled rather than how they looked. Remarkably, participants who played basketball themselves were better than non-players at recognizing the emotional expressions of the men labeled as players. Simply being told that another person was a fellow basketball player, whether that fact was true or not, enhanced their ability to interpret that person's emotions.[57]

Performance Anxiety

Work is one place in life where people experience regular assessments of their effectiveness. Evaluation is, for most people, an occasion for anxiety and uncertainty. Even those not prone to anxiety in other circumstances will get some butterflies when someone is judging them, implicitly or explicitly. In addition, it is all too apparent when star workers get more attention and recognition than average performers, yet another source of anxiety and resentment about employees' standing with their managers.

Forty-nine percent of employees with enough experience to become managers would turn down the spot if they had a chance. Working conditions are making people opt out; 82 percent consider increased stress a problem, 74 percent don't want to deal with disgruntled staff, 63 percent want to avoid paperwork, and 63 percent avoid the opportunity to manage so they never have to lay anyone off.[58]

> *Leaders must choose to be powerful instead of victims. The whole organization is watching them in terms of how they show up every day. If leaders convey a powerful form of personal leadership, it will help their people do the same.*
>
> —Randy Brown, chief human resources officer,
> WellPoint

Corporate Courage
Dr. Izzy Justice

I visited a large Fortune 200 company to process some challenging negative feedback that many middle managers had for their senior executives during their annual 360 Feedback Surveys. In talking with many of the senior executives, I discovered that they were convinced that their managers and leaders wanted the big title, the big role, the big compensation package, and the big office, but not the accountability that comes with it. They provided several examples of missed deadlines and mutually agreed-upon goals that were unmet by their middle managers.

My conversations with the middle managers, however, yielded a dramatically different perspective. They argued that senior leaders were setting unrealistic goals, and that they were being forced to achieve the kind of success that would be considered a tremendous accomplishment in times of abundant wealth, resources, and time. But they were expected to produce these results during a recession when they were also being asked to do more with less and were also in a gut-wrenching state of fear that inhibited risk-taking.

Which group is right? Should the senior executives not expect high levels of performance that would enable the company to emerge from the recession in a more efficient and healthier state of operating? Were the middle managers wrong to expect the time, resources, and proper goal setting necessary to achieve such lofty levels of performance? Both are equally fair requests. Yet, both parties played a role in creating their acrimonious situation.

The reality is that neither side wants to accept that they are both operating in an emotional situation akin to being held a "hostage." But to what are they being held hostage? Their personal fears and insecurities and their perceptions of past results and behaviors.

Further questioning uncovered a surprise consensus: both sides were deeply afraid of speaking up—they lacked the courage to ask meaningful questions, to challenge conventional wisdom, to explore new ideas, and to solicit outside support. This, to them, would be an implicit admission that they were either doing something wrong or were not competent enough.

Internal Competition

While the emerging workplace will rely more than ever on collaboration and teamwork, competition will always be a factor that has an impact on emotional safety.

> *Retail is a traditionally competitive industry.* "My store is winning and in the past, I didn't share why or how I was winning." *Now it's to the point that we can't afford managers to hoard knowledge. You have to share how and why your store is winning. So now it's healthy competition that allows for collaboration.*
>
> —Susan Richter, director of human resources, Food Lion, LLC

Workplaces have become bureaucratic, overly competitive, and emotionally unsafe. Humanity, intimacy, and compassion get lost in the process. When there is a sense of mutual humanity, the outcome will be trust and loyalty. And trust and loyalty open the doors to emotional safety, something we desperately need. Unfortunately, 31 percent of employees don't trust their boss.[59]

Emotional Labor

Some roles are tasked with the additional need to manage emotions so that they are consistent with organizational display rules,[60] regardless of whether they coincide with actual feelings. This may be for the purpose of customer service, investor relations, or simply pleasing the boss. Display rules[61] are organizational rules (spoken or unspoken) about what emotions are appropriate to exhibit at work. Research has shown a difference between surface acting and deep acting. Emotional labor is a form of emotional regulation where workers are expected to follow those display rules as a result of their job. Surface acting is simply "painting on" the emotion or faking the emotion without actually feeling or experiencing the emotion. This is associated with increased stress, emotional exhaustion and burnout, depression, and lack of authenticity. Deep acting, on the other hand, is when employees modify their real feelings and emotions to match the organization's expected or required emotional expression rules. This actually reduces stress and increases feelings of personal accomplishment.[62]

> *People are naturally emotional and need an outlet. When companies allow employees to express their emotions, relationships between people in an organization are better. Unfortunately, we are stuck in a belief system where people think of workplaces as cold, which results in a dysfunctional work environment. Managers at all levels should express and encourage the expression of emotions. When leaders express emotion, they are making an emotional connection with a person and that leads to genuine relationships.*
>
> —Leticia Knowles, American Express

Professional Status and Financial Stability

Employees' personal identities are often tied to their work. The fear of losing their job can cause many to feel unsafe doing what their better judgment, heart, and gut tell them to do. In addition, our companies compensate us for our time and effort, compensation which we then use to set a standard of living and establish our family's financial stability. Compromising these requires high levels of EQ and risk-taking that can have severe long-term consequences.

> *The courage to ask the why behind the how, the what, and the who starts with being very deliberate and committed as a leader to building trust in your department or your organization. To put this into action, demonstrate vulnerability with your folks. Practice full disclosure. Be open and candid. For example, I was having a conversation about something that didn't go as planned due to a mistake someone else made. I emphasized that I screw up a whole bunch of stuff, but the good news is I get more right than I get wrong. But I get a lot wrong too. That self-disclosure helps people see that it is okay to get things wrong and you won't lose your head.*
>
> —Kevin Henry, chief HR officer, Coca-Cola Bottling Consolidated C.

EMOTIONAL SAFETY

Leader: Kelli Price, senior vice president of people, Premier, Inc.
My overall mission is aligning business and employee performance.

Company:
Serving more than two thousand U.S. hospitals and more than fifty thousand other health-care sites, the Premier health care alliance and its members are transforming health care together. Nearly two hundred hospitals and health systems created and entirely own the Premier alliance. Premier's core purpose is "to improve the health of communities."

Premier's focus is on reducing costs, improving quality and safety, and managing people. Premier's ten- to thirty-year goal is that Premier's owners will be the leading health-care systems in their markets, and with them, Premier will be the major influence in reshaping health care.

Point of View:
In my early career, I emulated effective leaders. I investigated what made them successful. This sometimes worked and sometimes didn't. I realized that I needed to develop my own authentic style that allowed me to use my strengths and provided the freedom to fully engage others. I recognize that I will forever be developing and adapting my own personal leadership in order to be effective and support the needs of an ever-evolving business. As I have become less focused on myself and my need to do everything, I have found that people are much more eager to work together to achieve mutual success.

Best Practices:
Employees can't be authentic if they don't feel like it'll be respected. Organizations, in general, do not know how to support emotional safety. In order to change that, leadership must model emotional safety by being open and transparent. Make it known that it is okay to not always be right.

Lack of Emotional Safety: Impact on Organizations

Now that we know the causes of the lack of emotional safety in our organizations, we can ask, "What are the effects?" When emotional safety is not present, we are in a state that is more prone to a stress reaction. That means that the state of EPowerment is unattainable. When we feel at risk or on guard, we are more likely to take actions that will move us away from that state and back to a feeling of safety. We will sink further into our comfort zones, doing what we know how to do, and we will cease experimentation, innovation, risk-taking, and even collaboration.

> *Our change management team set out to find out how to manage change in the organization around the reduction of workforce, a result of the 2008–2009 recession. Employees were used to growth and now were faced with the opposite situation—a very different situation that was traumatic for employees at all levels. Many in the organization were in survival mode—not able to learn and develop. They were less concerned with self-actualization and self-development and more concerned about survival, personally and as a company. Some went into panic mode as a reaction to the new challenge and thus relied on what they knew. They became more reactive than proactive. In reflection, things may have gone differently. However, leaders took responsibility, and shouldered the burden.*
>
> —Linda Worden, director of training and organizational development, MeadWestvaco Corporation

Leaders have to become much more skillful and sensitive in creating emotional safety in the workplace. Unfortunately, many managers fail to recognize the lack of emotional safety and their personal impact on it. In many cases, this is simply more of an oversight or a lack in skill set than an explicitly desired state. No one wants an emotionally unsafe place, but no one is proactively doing things to make it safe either.

This can be understood, in part, as a lack of self-awareness on the part of many managers. Senior managers tend to overestimate their mastery of the skills and characteristics associated with emotional intelligence. The higher people rise in the ranks of management, the more they tend to rank themselves higher on emotional intelligence than their peers and direct reports rate them.

As people rise in management, they receive less and less coaching and direct feedback about their performance. And if they are doing something that affects the emotional safety of people who report to them, their people are highly unlikely to tell them about it. Lacking sufficient feedback, it is all too easy for managers to assume that they are much more adept at dealing with people than they might actually be. As a result, they keep doing things the way they always have without recognizing how they might be affecting the emotional safety and morale of the very people they are relying on to get things done. These are major EPowerment barriers.

A recent study asked people to rank ten places from an emotional and personal safety perspective. On the list were bars, homes, workplace, gyms, airports, etc. It was noted that the workplace ranked close to the bottom of list—even below bars. In other words, people feel emotionally safer in a bar than they do at work. While this may seem odd, it makes sense. The researchers inquired why people felt safer in a bar than they did at work. Respondents cited the workplace as a place where they had to be on their best behavior, in their best clothes, and performing at their best. The consequences for failing to do so can be severe, ranging from losing a job or being stereotyped to seeing opportunities and promotions go to other people.

> *Volvo makes safe products, and that carries over naturally into our culture. We have a consensus-driven culture where it is okay to challenge leadership, and as long as you do it respectfully, all ideas are heard.*
>
> —Troy Heflin, VP of organizational development, Volvo

Consider the effort it takes to prepare for work each day: wearing the right clothes, showing up and leaving at specific times, balancing work and life needs, and being constantly "on stage" in front of others, such as coworkers, bosses, and customers or clients. When Americans are spending longer hours at work than ever before, both physically and mentally, work can truly be an emotionally exhausting place. Contrast this to a bar. You show up and leave whenever you want. Alcohol loosens up the nerves and you take more risks with strangers. Perhaps you even yell, scream, and groove to the music. Little wonder that bars rated emotionally safer than workplaces.

There is additional research suggesting that the culprits in creating emotionally unsafe environments are not just the employers or leaders, but that we play a role in this ourselves. Our external characteristics, such as what we look like, our title, where we work, where our office space is, what we know and don't know, can serve as barriers to high performance just because of the story we tell ourselves internally. We may read a situation as prejudicial because we notice the gender or color of the people involved in the interaction. We may put undue pressure on ourselves if we haven't attained some level or status that a colleague working under very different circumstances in a very different department has.

Consider for a moment the role of work in our lives. Many of us base our self-worth on our perception of our professional competence and success. In addition, our stability and financial security is based on how well we are doing at work. Anything that even hints of a threat to our professional self-image and financial security affects our emotional security.

The key attribute required for substantive learning and in turn, high performance, is the ability to share what is truly on your mind. External characteristics cause us to revert to the instinctive fight-or-flight mode in lieu of emotionally safe and intellectually rational modes of learning. The fight-or-flight mode acts as a deterrent to EPowerment. Working adults today have built up huge defense mechanisms and shields to protect their image of themselves. That is a direct response to an emotionally unsafe environment. Yet, in the long term, these defense mechanisms and shields are more destructive than productive.

Consider how much effort it takes to be in a constant defensive mode versus a creative and high performing mode. A former NFL player offered a great perspective: "Our coach used to tell us that if we're not on the offense, someone else is moving the ball forward on us." Those with higher EQs are unquestionably moving the ball forward as they have figured out healthy balances between risk and reward and can intelligently leverage their skills to promote their gifts and talents. They have figured out a way to navigate through and cope with an unsafe environment.

If a company doesn't have emotional safety in its culture, the security base isn't there for all else to build upon. When people see instability, they become insecure, unless their leaders can handle their concerns with an EQ response. This inevitably will result in a severe drop in productivity. While companies may have been able to get away with an emotionally unsafe environment during the bad times, ultimately, the consequences are that people will leave the organization for a more supportive environment.

—Linda Worden, director of training and organizational development, MeadWestvaco Corporation

The role of emotional safety is central to creating an empowered organization. This is the mass and concerted use of emotional enablers. It is critical for a learner to feel emotionally safe while acquiring and practicing new skills so that old thinking and habits can be replaced with newer and better ones. Dee Hock, the founder of Visa, once said, "The problem is not how to get new, innovative thoughts into your mind, but how to get old ones out."

Recent research on workplace bullying provides yet more evidence of the critical role of emotional safety. In bullying workplaces, productivity is not affected in terms of quantity or quality. In fact people may work harder because they want to avoid being bullied. What does diminish are important behaviors associated with engagement, such as being nice to customers and engaging in humanizing behaviors with colleagues.[63] What also gets compromised severely is innovation within the organization.

Great ideas rarely start off great—they are random thoughts that are morphed into great ideas upon collaboration and validation with others. To squash those little seeds before they can blossom is the last thing that you want to do if you want to EPower your organization.

It is alarming how little attention we pay to the emotional state of employees. The recent recession felt like a hostage situation and it is virtually impossible to be creative and innovative and to perform highly in this state. The fear of losing one's job and the repercussions of perceptions of being ungrateful are barriers to EPowerment. A form of imbalance in the equilibrium of work has occurred and people know things are just going to be different.

> *One of my employees participating in a confidential online mentoring program[64] stated that he had an epiphany one day after concluding a virtual conversation with his anonymous mentor. He said, "Once I got comfortable with the idea of not knowing more details about my mentor I realized that the depth of our conversations was greater than I could possibly ever have in a face-to-face mentoring relationship." I think this is a true example of the power of emotional safety at work.*
>
> —Todd Harrison, director of leadership and associate development, WellPoint

---

EMOTIONAL SAFETY – BEST PRACTICES

1. Take the "emotional temperature" of both yourself and your staff every day.

2. Based on your reading, what immediate interventions can you induce to diffuse those powerful fears? You know yourself and your culture best.

3. Revisit what it means to be "empowered"—everyone has felt that at least once in their professional lives—what did it feel like then? What systems were in place that allowed you to be empowered? Make these lists and do not rest until they are manifested fully within your organization.

4. If we can list the things we do to make employees physically safe and to protect their property, let us list the things we do to make the workplace an emotionally safe workplace.

5. Create a culture of transparency and authenticity. Bring who you are into the workplace.

It takes emotional safety to buck bad trends, to seek the new, to ask the simple yet powerful questions, and to change the way you and other key stakeholders can effectively collaborate. It all starts with eliminating fear—that dreadful and invisible force we all know is presently around us.

> *Emotional safety should be central to your management and leadership development strategy. It is a key principle in achieving EPowerment and those high levels of performance we all seek. Emotional safety is also arguably the singular most important precursor for growing one's EQ, a key component of EPowerment. The good news is that with the e world, emotional safety is much easier to*

achieve. The Web can allow for deeper connections with others and can create a foundational structure that enables learning.

—Ruth Kennedy, director of organization
development, VF Corporation

Summary and Key Points

- Our physical safety is not at stake when we show up for work, but our emotional safety very well might be.
- Hierarchy, personal history, personality differences, value differences, diversity, performance anxiety, internal competition, emotional labor, and status can all play a role in creating an emotionally unsafe environment.
- Hierarchy can inhibit the formation of good working relationships between leaders and followers.
- Managers contribute to the lack of emotional safety because they lose awareness of their impact on people as they gain power.
- Differences between individuals pose a threat to emotional safety because of lack of understanding and lack of empathy.
- Performance anxiety and internal competition create a stressful atmosphere—an impediment to EPowerment.
- Emotional labor is a form of emotional regulation where workers are expected to display certain emotions and hold back others in order to do their job effectively or to meet organizational goals.
- Emotion is the core ingredient of a human being. People need an outlet for that, or it will be manifested through poor behavior or passive-aggressive actions.
- A culture without emotional safety will be a culture low on productivity and creativity.

Chapter 7
Mentoring

Mentoring can be wonderful. Getting to know someone where there are no distractions and encouraging a mentee to open up is like watching a flower unfold. Sometimes it is quick like a hothouse flower. Sometimes, it is hard for the mentee at first. Then you notice the communications becoming less guarded, more thoughtful and explorative. Suddenly, you realize that this person is sharing things with you they may not share with anyone else, at least not as openly. When you present a nonthreatening environment, there is a freedom to be yourself, rather than what those around you expect. It is a privilege to be part of each mentee's freedom.

Another valuable aspect, beyond the exercises, the challenges and the exchanges of ideas, is actually seeing a change—whether it's growth, a sudden recognition by the mentee, or perhaps a break-through in understanding. In particular, I remember a thread exchange where over time, the discussions moved away from how frustrating the mentee's team member was to considering what was motivating the team member's behavior to—and this is the great part—how the mentee could use that understanding of the team member's motivations and experience to encourage better communication and performance.

The relationships we develop are personal and special. I'm pleased that when my current mentee is frustrated or concerned about something, she'll use me as a sounding board. Even though she knows I'll ask questions, not give answers, she uses me to explore.

And while it shouldn't be a surprise, at the end you actually get to see measurable results. This is something you don't usually get with informal mentoring. The surprise isn't that the mentees have grown. You see it and know it from your interactions. It's that it can be measured. I'm convinced it offers value for both the mentees and the mentors in ways that traditional mentoring doesn't. And for me, this has been a very satisfying experience!

—Diane Adelberg, SPHR, operations
employment manager, Muzak LLC

The topic of mentoring generates divergent perspectives. There are many forms of mentoring, but at heart, mentoring is best defined in the classical sense of the term. The classical model is to learn from someone who has expertise and experience in doing what you are learning to do. Hundreds of years ago, if you wanted to be a carpenter, from whom did you learn? A carpenter, of course. You would hardly go to the town mayor or the blacksmith, no matter how old or wise the latter was.

> *Mentoring is often misunderstood and not presented effectively. What happens is usually the company identifies a mentor and the needs. But mentoring is dynamic. One can have multiple mentors—a technical mentor, an EQ mentor, an on-boarding mentor. Mentoring can't be prescribed. It must be embraced by employees who understand their developmental areas.*
>
> —Effenus Henderson, chief diversity officer,
> Weyerhaeuser

Historically, there is tremendous power in the classical model. In the contemporary world, such guidance is often employed where peak performance, our ultimate goal, is at a true premium. If you look at athletics and professional sports, you will find that the coach of an NBA basketball team is someone who played basketball and has spent a significant portion of his life in basketball—not someone who played soccer. In Olympic athletics, coaches have spent a lifetime in the field that the young athlete is trying to master. And indeed, these athletes perform at world-class performance levels on some of the grandest stages in front of millions. Learning constantly, a cornerstone of the EPowerment model, from someone who has been there and done that and has lived through all the successes and failures inherent in the journey, adds instant credibility, creates instant context and actually induces the learner to want to learn more.

I have a coaching style, which I learned from great leaders in my past who pushed me and saw capabilities in me that I didn't know I had and provided me with stretch opportunities that allowed me to learn and grow. It built my confidence and now I try to do the same for my employees by setting high expectations and coaching them through.

—Troy Heflin, VP of organizational development, Volvo

So why don't we follow the same model for working professionals as we do for these athletes who seek to perform at their best constantly? Aren't working professionals also paid for their performance? Seemingly, the workplace has accepted as fact that most employees will be mediocre and can't all possibly be superstars. Yet identifying someone as a superstar can make him or her a superstar, and placing a different label on someone can create a self-fulfilling prophecy that limits success. So it has happened that many professionals themselves have also accepted as fate that they are simply going to be average. Their apathy is perhaps driven by the aforementioned reasons empowerment failed.

While companies do provide coaching for executives, there are some fundamental differences between coaching and mentoring. First, coaching is often reserved for top executives while mentoring is provided for middle managers. Second, coaching is usually seen as an intervention, meaning that coaches are hired to "fix" some flaw of an executive. Mentoring, on the other hand, is based on a wellness model: there is nothing "wrong" with the mentee that needs to be fixed but the mentee will benefit from a relationship with someone who is willing to share expertise and experience. And the mentor usually benefits as well!

Harvard Business Review asked 140 leading executive coaches about their work and found that, in recent years, the reasons companies engage coaches have changed. Ten years ago, most companies called coaches in to help fix toxic behavior at the top. Today, most coaching aims to develop the capabilities of top performers.[65]

The most frequent reason for hiring executive coaches is to boost the performance of high potential leaders. Ninety-three percent of leaders who have worked with a coach considered the experience a success.[66]

> *To deal with an undesired behavior, send the person to coaching. A supportive environment provides the best probability for the person to understand the impact of the behavior.*
>
> —Steve Larson, Senior VP of diversity, engagement, and inclusion, Wells Fargo

> *To deal with an undesired behavior, validate their emotions first and respect their needs and rights. Then, provide a forum for expressing emotions in a healthy, safe, and appropriate way. Healthy boundaries will set the stage for appropriate responses.*
>
> —Leticia Knowles, American Express

Coaches are usually generalists and may never have worked in their clients' industry or served in the positions held by their clients. Mentors, on the other hand, are drawn from the industry and have experience in roles similar to their mentees. There are exceptions to these differences and there is some overlap between mentoring and coaching. Nonetheless, these distinctions are important to note in the context of optimizing human performance.

While this may come across as bias against coaches, please don't take it as such. Many executives credit coaches for helping them overcome a flaw that they have had for years. Coaching is a great model when behavioral change is needed, in those cases where we need assistance from someone more formal than a friend or colleague but the issue at hand is not quite severe enough to warrant psychotherapy. There is a place for interventions and for executive coaching, but these solutions are expensive and not very scalable in achieving EPowerment throughout an organization. Coaching tends to be face-to-face or via phone at pre-determined times, whereas newer mentoring models serving a tech-savvy workforce can be done online and asynchronously, making it easier to reach thousands of mentees without the barriers of scheduling and geography.

> *Love and caring are elements of a good mentoring relationship. Negativity is a reality of organizational life. Mentoring is a kind of caring that individuals feel for others that make them want to help them.*
>
> —Bill Hodgetts, VP of corporate leadership development, Fidelity

Mentoring will become even more appealing in the workforce of 2010 and beyond as baby boomers begin their migration out of the workplace and are replaced by younger generations. The younger generation reports that mentoring is the preferred model for workplace learning. It is appealing to learn from someone who has achieved what they are setting out to achieve. "In our focus groups, employees are screaming for networking and mentoring; they want people to teach them effectiveness and business skills," says Anne Feller of Cox Communications.

Members of Generation Y often seek out baby boomers as mentors, in part because of their cultural proximity to their own parents and shared values. In addition, Gen Y'ers and boomers engage in reverse mentoring, helping boomers master technology for optimal performance. boomers, in turn, help the Gen Y'ers with good old-fashioned wisdom. For example, Time Warner has a program called Digital Reverse Mentoring. Interns and entry-level employees mentor senior executives on emerging digital trends such as Facebook, Twitter, and other Web 2.0 applications and how they are used.[67]

Classical mentoring in the form of apprenticeships disappeared because the human race grew in size and then geographically dispersed across the world. To find a person wherever you lived or worked who had done what you wanted to do became challenging. And in the past twenty-five years, the constant change in jobs and roles also meant that there might be no available people who had done what you are trying to be the best at. With the advent of the Web and devices that can now connect us to new people, communities, and sources of knowledge, the definition of mentoring itself can now be revisited.

Mentoring at Leading Companies

At **Black & Decker**, we have a formal mentoring program that has gone through three flights, for eight months, at about twenty to twenty-two people per flight. Over sixty employees have gone through this program in the past three years. We solicit volunteers but give preference to the high potentials. It has worked wonders for internal networking, trusting relationships, a cross-functional perspective, and more connectivity as well as visibility across the organization. As we all know, there are formal structures, but then things really get done based on the informal relationships that develop in an organization. We find that, at the end of the eight months, these relationships tend to continue on an informal basis.

We use mentoring for individualized development rather than programmatic development at **Fidelity**. In line with decades of psychology and mentoring research, we encourage leaders to create constellations of relationships with multiple mentors addressing different needs.

Cox Communications has a mentor network on their intranet site. Employees who are looking for a mentor access it, answer a series of questions, and walk away with a list of mentor matches and their contact information. Potential mentees contact one or two people from that list. The outcome depends on the structure of the specific mentoring relationship. If the mentors have a process for what they are doing, it goes extremely well. If it's simply used as a resume builder, the relationship doesn't work for long. To make it more impactful, Cox encourages a servant leadership style—as a mentor, ask yourself, "How can I be more service oriented rather than content driven?"

Redefining Mentoring

Mentoring is not an outcome. It is a process. Historically, the desired goal was to transfer experience, knowledge, and wisdom from people who had it to those who needed it. Consider a change in this model. In today's world, should it really matter who the sources of the experiences, knowledge, and wisdom may be? Whether they are internal or external to your company? Whether it comes from a person or a community or a knowledge source? The key here is not the distinction between the "source" of the knowledge needed to make the better decisions for high performance. In today's e world, what has changed is accessibility to knowledge and wisdom from anywhere, from any source and most importantly, at the time that you need it so that you can make a better decision and convert those learning moments into *aha!* moments more frequently.

Consider a new definition of mentoring to be "a process designed to provide access to knowledge from wherever it exists, whether from a person, a community, or a source of knowledge, to whoever needs it at the time they need it." If mentoring is a process, then the outcome under the new definition is an EPowered individual, capable of attaining high performance.

> *Mentoring and coaching, which, in my opinion exist on the same spectrum, are about the development of someone. That accountability to another (the mentor or coach) makes the learning stick. Whatever you call the method, it can be an accelerant in setting up a team for success as they go, especially as you are trying to move to a new culture, structure, or process.*

> —Jane Luciano, VP of global learning and organization development at Bristol-Myers Squibb

Individuals and organizations are now positioned to take advantage of the new world—a world in which technology and connectivity have eliminated geography as a barrier to finding a mentor. People are already connecting with friends and family online. EPowerment is already in motion. The workplace has to catch up quickly or seriously risk losing the high performers and those who want to be high performers to others.

MENTORING

Leader: Susan Richter, director of human resources, Delhaize/ Food Lion, LLC

Company:
Delhaize America is a leading supermarket operator in the United States with over fifteen hundred stores in sixteen states in the eastern United States. Delhaize America operates under the banners Food Lion, Bloom, Bottom Dollar, Harveys, Hannaford Bros., and Sweetbay, each of which has a distinct strategy and a well-established brand image. Delhaize America employs approximately 109,000 full-time and part-time associates up and down the East Coast. Food Lion reorganized as a holding company, Delhaize America, in 1999 to promote flexibility in the management of each distinct banner.

Point of View:
I rarely say someone works for me; we work together. We meet as a team and one-on-one. One-on-one is about building people up and helping them in the work they are doing. I stretch people on my team. I encourage my team members to do research on the latest trends and best practices, and then we share knowledge: they share their findings and I share what we did on that topic historically, and then we collaborate to work out a strategy for the future. I ask a lot of questions rather than coming up with the answers. I don't get riled up if there is a deadline and something blows up. We do talk about what happened and learn from it. As a result, people feel motivated after they meet with me. I have been told I have a calming, yet motivating effect.

Best Practices:
- **External Mentoring:** External mentoring at Food Lion takes the form of pairing high potentials or those who need improvement with an external mentor.

MENTORING

- **Informal Mentoring:** But there is a lot of informal mentoring—in an "I would like to gain insight from you" way, and those sessions may last three days or three years. Employees just have to have the guts to ask a senior leader to do that—and they rarely say no.
- **Group Mentoring:** In 2009, we kicked off learning partner teams. Learning partners are groups of people whom you don't work with every day. The purpose is to gain new perspectives and stretch your mind. There are three guiding principles for learning partners:

  1. Explore—explore new possibilities, be curious about yourself and others;

  2. Serve—how am I serving those I am a learning partner with? Confidentiality, empathy and reliability all help create a safe place to learn;

  3. Inspire—Know that your sharing is a gift. Your feedback is a gift. How am I inspiring others on my team and how am I inspired by them?

     Use at least a trio, because three people can bond more easily than two people. With just two people, it may become an adversarial relationship.

- **Self-Mentoring:** Learn on your own, using all available tools.
- **Feedback:** Knowledge sharing and feedback allows us to learn much faster and in a higher quantity than in the past. We have used too much directive feedback in the past. Now we are moving toward including more inspirational feedback vs. intimidation feedback.
- **Peer Mentoring:**If someone goes to a training session, they come back and share that knowledge with the team. At our meetings, we have "thought partner conversations."

The Critical Role of Experience

There's been considerable discussion over the years about experience and how powerful of a performance enabler it can be. If you listen to seasoned athletes who have played their sport for some time and are asked what advantage they have over a newcomer or a younger, more athletic person or team, the response is invariably—experience. When people in the workplace are hired or promoted, one of the more critical elements for that hire or promotion is that the person "has experience," and, as a result of that experience, they are often compensated much more than those with less experience.

So what exactly is experience? Two men can truthfully say that they have been truck drivers for ten years. Yet one of them drove once a month for ten years and the other drove every week for ten years. Would the experience of the latter be more relevant in mentoring a new truck driver? Of course it would. So experience cannot be simplified to a number. And as such, just being older does not a mentor make. So what is it then?

It is estimated that the average human being has about eighty substantive experiences a year. A substantive experience is one that has the potential to provide insight, wisdom, or personal growth. These eighty experiences present us opportunities to learn and generate major *aha!* moments. Yet, the average person only processes an average of three of those eighty experiences a year. Without processing the experience, that is, without taking the time to reflect on what we might learn from that experience, the potential wisdom to be gained from the event is lost.

When we leave over 96 percent of our significant learning moments on the table, major opportunities are lost. This also means that the benefits of the aforementioned "level of experience" could be significantly enhanced if we took the time to process more of our experiences. If we were to reflect more and learn more from our experiences, we would develop wisdom much earlier. For example, if we were to double our average to six, starting at age thirty, it is arguable that by age forty we would have the experience, and EQ, of a fifty-year-old—ten years earlier.

Without processing and learning from our experiences, we are missing out on great opportunities to learn from life, and thus we are missing out on living a much richer and fulfilling life. This is one of the more powerful ways to increase your EQ as well. Processing an experience means to reflect on it, discuss it with someone objective, figure out the lessons, see how others have handled it, and make a proactive plan to integrate those lessons in your life. And if you can process all this at the time you are experiencing any one of those eighty substantive experiences, you are surely increasing your EQ and empowering yourself as a learner and as a high performer.

The online environment has created forums for more of these eighty experiences to be processed. Because you can access multiple sources from literally anywhere, unlike any other time in history, EPowerment has never been more achievable.

Organizations that embrace mentoring, in the traditional or contemporary models, or in the redefined model that encompasses and allows for both, are going to have greater collective wisdom as their employees were able to convert more learning moments to *aha!* moments. Mentoring is a powerful enabler for the substantive growth that the working professional needs and wants—the type of growth that enables EPowerment.

Summary and Key Points

- Mentoring is a process, not an outcome.
- The classical model of mentoring is learning from someone who has achieved the very thing you want to do.
- The benefits of mentoring are learning from someone who has been there and done that and has lived through all the successes and failures inherent in the journey.
- Coaching and mentoring are distinct activities.
- Coaching is reserved for executives and behavioral change attempts, while mentoring is a wellness model that can be utilized by anyone.
- Younger generations have a desire to develop themselves through mentoring.
- All experiences are not equal. Substantive experiences present an opportunity for growth.
- To receive the benefits of experiences, a person must process and digest the experiences.
- Classical apprenticeship, an early form of mentoring, disappeared because the human race grew in size and then we geographically dispersed across the world.

Chapter 8
Multi-Mode Learning

A North Carolina elementary school with a high poverty level and minority population moved from the thirtieth percentile in reading and math on the California Achievement Test to the eighty-third percentile in three years. The only change at that school was the introduction of learning-styles instruction.[68] *Learning-styles instruction takes into account the different needs and preferences of the learner that affect knowledge acquisition. Specifically, research shows that learners are affected by the following*[69]:

1. *Their immediate environment (sound, light, temperature, and furniture and seating design).*

2. *Their own emotionality (motivation, persistence, responsibility—conformity or nonconformity—and the need for either externally imposed structure or the opportunity to do things their own way).*

3. *Sociological preferences (learning alone, in a pair, in a small group, as part of a team, with an authoritative*

or collegial adult, and wanting variety as opposed to patterns and routines).

4. *Physiological characteristics (perceptual strengths, time-of-day energy levels, and need for intake or mobility while learning).*

5. *Processing inclinations (global or analytic; right brain or left brain; and impulsive or reflective).*

Multi-mode learning is also referred to as blended learning. Blended learning was defined in a recent issue of *Chief Learning Officer* magazine as "executing a learning strategy that integrates multiple delivery modalities (both synchronous and asynchronous) and, in doing so, creating the best possible solution for your target audience."[70]

When you were in college, some of your knowledge came via the professor during lecture, some came from reading the textbook, some came from doing the homework assignments, some came from project work, some came from cramming the night before, and—if you're from Gen Y—some came from Googling. Some of what you learned may not have struck you until you got your first job and you realized *that's* what they were talking about. Some students utilized all of these modalities while others were insistent on learning just through one specific way—such as reading the textbook and skipping the class.

Similarly, when you show up at work on a Monday morning, the best way for you to learn at that time may be to read an article. On Tuesday morning, you may prefer to talk with someone. On Wednesday, you might watch a video. On Thursday you might learn from collaborating in a team environment. And Friday's learning needs may call for accessing large amounts of information via a database of best practices, case studies, and research.

Our learning needs change quickly and are dictated by factors such as events in the workplace, our moods, style, and the context of those learning moments. The more modalities of learning that are available to us, the higher the probability that we will pick one that is applicable to us at that specific point in time and is relevant to meet our specific need.

We must make learning more accessible, including learning on-demand, e-learning, global systems, etc. People need info that they can easily and conveniently pull up at the point of transaction, with step-by-step instructions to help when they need it. That on-demand capability puts into learners' hands the opportunity to pull learning as they need, and technology allows for that.

—Jane Luciano, VP of global learning and development, Bristol-Myers Squibb

Multi-mode learning is consistent with the 70-20-10 Model of Learning that asserts that 10 percent of job-related learning takes place in the classroom, 20 percent is experiential learning, and the lion's share, 70 percent, comes from addressing challenging workplace challenges on the job, in real time, as they occur. This model came about soon after 1999, when the Department of Labor estimated that 70 percent of learning occurs informally.

This is consistent with the fact that learning moments are so unpredictable and transient. When we fail to process these learning moments, the probability of recapturing them at a future time is very low. We tend to move on to the next experience, the next task at hand—and the opportunity is lost entirely.

If most of our workplace learning (90 percent)[71] supposedly happens while we are working, the multi-mode learning principle is all the more relevant because it is the kind of learning that occurs to meet emerging needs on the job.

We all learn differently. Personality differences, motivators, and previous experience with the content all interact to create a unique personal learning style. Extraverts may prefer collaborative learning in a face-to-face atmosphere. Assertive individuals may clarify their thought through a stimulating debate. Introverts may find their learning moment as they reflect on their own thoughts after writing them down. Visual learners may need to see a video before the new information clicks.

> *There are three components to the blended, extended, high-potential leadership development program we call "Invest in the Best" at WellPoint. First, our action learning model helps employees self-reflect on learnings and consider how they might apply the newly acquired knowledge to their job. Second, employees are provided with a coach and/ or a mentor—and we view those two differently at WellPoint. Third, there is an opportunity to work on "stretch" project assignments. These are cohort-based and centered on a current business initiative. The cohorts get a team coach and a business sponsor and are debriefed at several stages of the project, so it becomes an iterative learning process as opposed to a singular event.*
>
> —Todd Harrison, director of leadership and associate development, WellPoint

MULTI-MODE LEARNING

Leader: Ruth Kennedy, director of organization development, VF Corporation

Ruth revised VF Corporation's global performance management process and implemented best practices for talent management across the organization. Her role focuses on senior-level talent development and succession management.

Company:

VF Corporation is a highly diversified global supply chain and values its customer first. VF strategy begins with a passion for the products and a deep understanding of consumers—the art and science of apparel. VF also boasts a perpetually driven culture focused on constant innovation. VF Corporation employs 46,000 people in 150 countries.

VF Corporation brands include Wrangler, 7 For All Mankind, Lee, Nautica, Jansport, Reef, and The North Face just to name a few. To give customers the best experience possible and to be able to build long-term relationships, it is imperative to have the most skilled people in every position throughout the organization. VF Corporation's revenue is over $7 billion.

Point of View:

People are your greatest value proposition; if leaders can provide the relationship and the structure, employees will inevitably grow. Everyone has an inner purpose and a unique passion. An understanding that we are all wired differently will maximize potential in others. Know who they are and what value they add, no matter their level.

MULTI-MODE LEARNING

Best Practices:
To create the most effective learning environment, organizations can't rely on just one modality. One way of learning may not be enough for an individual. A learning method that engages a more visual and conceptual learner may not do so for a kinetic or auditory learner. It needs to be supplemented. But too many options can sometimes be a burden. It's like a large cocktail party: the learner is not sure where to begin. The trick is to see where they connect with the content. As a learner, look for the place where you belong so you can get a lot out of it.

A best practice in implementing innovative learning solutions is to leverage mavens, salesmen, and connectors. There will be some who are wildly engaged from the start. There will be some that are adamantly resistant from the start. Then there will be some in the middle. Those who are using it and seeing benefits can sway, teach, and engage that middle group, increasing your chance for success.

Providing Options

It is incumbent on organizations to provide a wide array of easily accessible modalities of learning so that the learners will simply and easily pick the right one for them. Making various modalities readily available will accommodate diversity in learning styles and ensure that people capitalize on otherwise transient learning moments. It will also provide the experience of EPowerment when the employees realize that the power to solve any problem is literally at their fingertips. It is virtually impossible to predict what modality will be the best for each employee, so the more modalities you have, the more easily this will occur.

Does it enhance training? Does it cut costs? The answer has to be yes to both! Get people out of hotels and restaurants. The original solution for that was computer-based training. Now we have the ability for more unique solutions. Seventy to 90 percent of training in our organization is informal training, and our question becomes, "How can we best support that?"

—VP of training and development at a major
retail chain

Learning Styles

Reading (visual)
Listening (auditory)
Seeing (visual)
Speaking (auditory)
Doing (Tactile/Kinesthetic)

Multi-mode learning is intuitive and well-supported empirically. But how can an organization provide so many modes of learning? In a world where Web 1.0, 2.0, and now 3.0 have gained traction, multi-mode learning has never been easier to orchestrate. Unfortunately, many organizations have not yet taken advantage of the power of technology and the exponential growth in accessibility and platforms. In practical terms, maximizing learning and productivity modalities can only occur by leveraging the best of today's technologies.

For example, TED.com has created popular ten- to twenty-minute videos that are simply awe-inspiring and give everyone unprecedented access to some amazing people whom we otherwise would have never met or known. YouTube is another rich source of information. Sixty-two percent of adult Web users watch videos on online sharing sites like YouTube, compared with 33 percent in December 2006. Eighty-nine percent of eighteen to twenty-nine year-old Web users watch videos on video-sharing sites; 36 percent watch such videos daily.[72] Yet, many companies block external Web site access and even penalize those who try to access outside sources of knowledge.

Research and knowledge repositories housing case studies, articles, and best practices are also available with the click of a mouse. These repositories house knowledge and wisdom that traditionally existed only within consulting firms. Wikipedia is a great example of a place to find quick facts and knowledge that again add to the modality of learning. And in the case of Wikipedia, the latest numbers show that it is actually more accurate than Britannica.[73] Who needs to go to the library anymore? With access to powerful search engines, finding what you want has also never been easier.

Surprisingly, instead of facilitating the use of these technologies, many companies block access to them. Fifty-four percent of employers ban access to social networks; 19 percent of companies allow social networking use only for business purposes, and just 16 percent allow limited personal use.[74] Blocking access to sites is counterproductive—employees aren't able to consult the resources they have become accustomed to using. In some workplaces, even the local university library Web site is blocked. Furthermore, social networking technologies are fast becoming a way to do business, reach new markets, and satisfy current customers.

What are organizations afraid of? Workers who engage in Workplace Internet Leisure Browsing (WILB) are more productive than those who don't.[75] And it's not a select few, either. In fact, 70 percent of people who use the Internet at work engage in WILB.[76] Employees who spend some of their work day browsing and Googling, as long as it's not excessive, are 9 percent more productive than those who don't.

We have an attention span of no more than twenty minutes. We need breaks to remain productive. It is ironic that companies spend millions on technologies that block and inhibit the productivity and creativity that they preach is so important to their organization. Social community technologies have become a new way to do business. The assumption is that an employee engaging in online shopping or scanning Facebook pages is less productive. This is a fundamental flaw in how we measure productivity.

When working on a complex task, we need to disengage from it to let the brain work on it. If you recall from the last chapter, this is why the Extended Learning Model works so well. Disengaging may mean taking a walk, playing a video game, or surfing the Internet. During these breaks, our brain is at work, just like when we are sleeping, processing the information and finding new relationships while sorting through seemingly unrelated data. This is why we have some of our best insights in those moments when we are doing something completely different, and, suddenly, an idea or solution to a problem jumps into our minds.

A leading generations expert, Hayden Shaw,[77] is fond of telling this story: A manager approached him after one of his presentations, concerned that he was about to make a bad decision regarding the firing of an employee for "generational reasons." He explained that the young employee had been put on notice for spending as much as three hours a day in Workplace Internet Leisure Browsing.

When asked by Mr. Shaw if this WILB was cutting into

this employee's productive time at work, the manager said no, adding that, as a matter of fact, the person was actually the most productive person on the team. When asked if this employee was accessing "forbidden" Web sites, the manager also said that, no, the sites visited were online shopping, social networking, or news sites. Ultimately, the story ends with the manager realizing that the only reason he had considered firing the person was that he thought it set a bad example for the rest of the workforce. After talking through the situation with Hayden Shaw, the manager came to the realization that this person should not only *not* be fired but should instead be held up as an example of someone who was more productive because of the fact that he could stay connected through his WILB activities.

Learning Innovations

VF Corporation has a blended strategy which includes e-learning, classes, and research articles, as well as online tools for managers. People can be resistant to things with an e-component if that is not the way they live their lives. The trick to overcoming that resistance is to show them how to use the e-tools and how they can leverage this knowledge for their business roles. It is imperative to establish both a reason for learning and the context for learning. Answer the question, "Why am I doing this?" and employees will be more engaged in their learning and development.

Training needs can be broken down into smaller pieces. Everyone is an expert at something. **MeadWestvaco Corporation** has a few Excel wizards who educate employees who have a need to learn about Excel. Experts identify what training they could do, and a schedule of one to two topics per week is created. Employees sign themselves up for training sessions—the benefit of this is that people sign up for exactly what they need. The strategy is to bring people together, and the most effective trainers are the subject-matter experts themselves. Trainers work with them to create materials and facilitate effectively.

WellPoint uses "e-nags" that are instant advice modules that provide a post-session resource for the employees. They come with suggestions and keep the topic fresh in employees' minds.

Accessing Experiential Knowledge

Accessibility connects us to not only explicit and functional knowledge but to experiential wisdom as well. Human connections lead to unprecedented levels of insight and knowledge generation. We can easily connect to a second ear, a wall to bounce an idea off of, or a support system not otherwise available. We can easily connect to new people who are experts at what they do. We can also connect to new communities of experts or collaborators who are well outside of the traditional boundaries of our own company, geography, and area of expertise. The idea of cross-industry collaboration is gaining tremendous popularity, as some industries are better at certain dimensions of work than others. Six Sigma, the very popular management process, for example, started in the manufacturing industry as a quality initiative and today, industries like health care have adopted it for care of services—but it took over twenty years before it found its way to health care.

> *We are focusing on adaptive, Internet-based technologies focused on core competencies. Learning occurs in a variety of venues. There will be a transformation in the future, where large organizations will be connected, but not as one company. The learning function must have agility to deal with that; it must be prepared to move and change as an organization changes. Agree on outcomes, and the details will work themselves out.*
>
> —Effenus Henderson, chief diversity officer,
> Weyerhaeuser

Online collaboration sites are also popular. Why not throw an idea out there and get help for it from dozens of your peers? In very short periods of time, the idea morphs into an actual solution for an issue facing the organization. Compare this to the traditional "suggestion boxes" that companies had at certain locations in their buildings. This evolved to a few companies creating suggestion box e-mail accounts, but even these are archaic compared with the possibilities that exist today. Wikis, the collaborative websites that anyone can edit, have turned into a powerful co-creation modality where knowledge and ideas are worked on collectively, in real or asynchronous time, from the convenience of a cell phone or laptop, wherever an employee is. What is the possibility that, whatever you are working on now, someone, somewhere in the world, in whatever industry, has already either done it or is doing it concurrently? The probability is very high if you think about it. Why not leverage this collective human knowledge? How satisfying and empowering could it be to take an idea or a project and do it better the first time around than was traditionally possible? Why not take an idea that was executed the first time in a mediocre fashion and make it excellent? This is EPowerment. This is harnessing the capacity of available technologies and concurrently developing one's emotional acumen by converting more learning moments. This is, simply, high performance.

Various Learning Modalities	
• Video clips	• Lecture
• E-learning modules	• Podcast
• Articles	• Presentation
• Books	• Workshop
• Blogs	• Conference
• Case studies	• Webinar
• Best practices	• Simulations
• Peer mentoring	• Industry trends report
• Traditional one-to-one mentoring	• Games
• On-the-job training	• Action learning
• On-boarding	• Informal/continuous learning
• Diversity training	• Collaboration
• Training for skills and competencies	• Project teams
• Degree education	• Stretch assignments
• Certificate programs from institution	• Quiz/Examination
• Discussion group	• Industry trends on Twitter
• Book club	• Self-learning and self-exploration
• Coaching	• Magazines
• Chatting	• Journals
• From Subject Matter Experts	• Teleconference

These best practices can now be experienced in real time. The onus is clearly on chief learning officers and leaders of every organization to seek multiple modes of learning for their employees so that they can make the best possible decisions at the time that they need to be made. Isn't this what empowerment was supposed to be?

The core concept behind multi-mode learning is that there is no single best way to learn. An organization that prides itself in one or two ways of training and developing its people, especially if it focuses on classroom learning, is going to lose to other companies that take advantage of the growth in the available modalities of learning. It is already happening (see the insert on page 145, Learning Innovations). The barriers to collective human knowledge are collapsing as we speak. But this is good news. There is nothing to be afraid of if one of your employees seeks to take advantage of it. You should take advantage of it.

The treasure chest is not knowledge alone, but the execution of that knowledge. Everyone in this world sees the swing that Tiger Woods has. It is dissected every time he plays and is right there for any aspiring golfer to copy. But no one has. He is the only one who does what he does. Yet, many of us pick up one or two things about him that can improve our game too. Luckily, there has never been a better time to be in a career, as the ability to reach one's highest potential and perform at very high levels has never been more achievable. Through multiple modalities, we are all a step closer to realizing EPowerment.

Summary and Key Points

- There is no single best way to learn, and people vary in their preferred style of learning.
- Our individual learning needs also change from day to day.
- To capitalize on learning moments, make multiple modalities readily accessible.
- Online learning is limitless and full of potential.
- Organizations block access to one of the most powerful and efficient performance enablers we have ever seen: the Web.
- Cross-industry collaboration prevents reinventing the wheel and makes innovation faster.
- Multiple modalities can refer to knowledge sources, diverse experiences, and varied points of view.
- The more learning modalities that are available, the higher the chance that we learn something!
- Technology now makes knowledge and wisdom available at the point of need.

Chapter 9
Outcome-Based Learning

HR people try to perpetuate the idea that job satisfaction is critical, but there is no evidence that engaging employees impacts financial returns. The language of organizations is numbers, and HR isn't very good at data analytics. They don't think like business people. Many of them entered human resources because they wanted to help people, which I'm all for, but I'm also for building winning organizations.

—Richard Beatty, director of Rutgers University's Master in Human Resource Leadership Program, at the CFO Rising conference in Orlando, Fla.

In the past five years, HR has been enjoying the greatest power it has ever had. The "war for talent," which companies have fought tooth and nail, will be over in 2008, neither lost nor won: there will be a ceasefire brought on by lack of funds and exhaustion of the troops. An old truth will be whispered by the brave: most workers are not terribly talented and most of them don't need to be, as most jobs don't require it. In 2009, a more elitist shift will occur: companies will worry about the performance of those at the top of the pyramid, while everyone else will be managed like a commodity. "Talent" will be a word we wave good-bye to. In 2009, the word "staff" will make a comeback, as will "head count."[78]

—The Year of the CFO, The Economist

First, to understand and differentiate the concept of outcome-based learning, let's compare it to continuous learning. Continuous learning is great: it's the notion that we learn each day and are open to new and divergent ideas and perspectives. There is overwhelming research showing that those of us who continuously develop new skills are not only more productive at work, but also significantly happier in life. The continuous learning model keeps boredom away and competition at bay. To this end, professional training and development companies and consultants have had very successful runs. Internal learning and development programs have also flourished, with many companies even creating internal "universities" offering all kinds of skill-based learning programs. Many companies have chief learning officers in place to lead this continuous learning model. But this is not what outcome-based learning is all about; in fact, continuous learning is part of the extended learning models principle.

Outcome-based learning is about connecting learning

activities to a concrete, work-related outcome. When experimental research is done in psychology, scientists first do something important that can make or break the results of their experiment: they operationalize their variables. This means that they take a conceptual view of the subject they want to study and put it in terms that can be measured. For example, "growth" is a fuzzy term. If a researcher wants to operationalize "growth," the researcher must specify how growth is measured (height vs. weight,) define what measure will be used, state how and when measurements will be made, and explain what constitutes significant growth vs. trivial growth. Outcome-based learning is about operationalizing your learning.

> *When the individual is responsible for his or her own personal development, and that growth is supported by the organization; when there is a connection between learning and business outcomes; and when the leadership team understands the value proposition to not only the employee but also the clients, you truly have a learning organization.*
>
> —Effenus Henderson, chief diversity officer,
> Weyerhaeuser

It is not enough just to learn something, attend a class, or ace an exam. Tie the new learning to a tangible and relevant result, goal, or outcome.

> *To operationalize learning, ask yourself what you are going to do differently tomorrow. At Fidelity, we make sure that happens in a couple of different ways:*

- *Action learning is built into leadership development programs.*

- *We ensure leaders have robust, specific, and relevant development plans—plans that aren't aspirational goals but instead are operationalized to their day-to-day work.*

- *Coaches assist our senior leaders with crafting operational and actionable development plans.*

—Bill Hodgetts, VP of corporate leadership development, Fidelity

When you finish a class, workshop, or Webinar, you get these little forms they want you to fill out: "Did you enjoy the speaker today?" "How helpful will this be on the job for you? (Rank 1-5; 1=not at all helpful, 5=very helpful)"

While enjoying the class may be an important component of engagement, there is no correlation between learner satisfaction and impact to business.[79] This means that there is no relationship between learners saying they loved the presenter or the content or they thought they learned something, and there being an actual positive impact on the business as a result of that learning.

We measure reactions because it is easy, but the end-of-session evaluation forms—the standard practice in training rooms all over the world—turn out to be one of the worst possible ways to measure the impact of what you have learned. These evaluation forms cannot measure whether the learner actually learned something or that the learning resulted in some positive impact to the business of the learner. In fact, reported reactions to training are largely affected by instructor teaching style (most important!), individual trainee characteristics (personality, disposition, emotional state, motivation, organizational commitment, etc.), organizational support for the training initiative, and the level of human interaction involved in the training.[80]

When the desired results are not achieved, human development professionals turn their attention to changing the content or figuring out better ways to present the data in lieu of figuring out how the learning can directly impact the business by addressing a business issue. Most companies have, in the past decade or so, realized that people are their most important asset and they invest in their employees—just take a look at the "About Us" section on any leading corporate Web page. Yet, there is a disconnect. As we have seen in recent times, a tough financial situation inevitably leads to budget cuts and almost always, training and development budgets get cut first. The reason for this is that it is not clear to the executives, and CFOs in particular, how continuous learning impacts their business. To those outside of the human capital profession, it is not very intuitive that in tough times, the right answer is actually to invest more in professional development so that new ideas are explored and harnessed, and therefore can manifest necessary business changes which can help the company get out of the downturn faster and come out better prepared for the new business climate.

> *At WellPoint, we have been asked by our business managers to show them the return on investment they will get from any particular learning solution we provide before they invest the money. Since in-depth ROI studies are expensive, we have taken full advantage of predictive analytics to demonstrate, in a reasonable and structured manner, the impact of our learning events in eight key performance*

indicators areas, including ROI. In using a logical, systematic approach we were able to present business leaders with data that they deemed good enough for them to feel comfortable in making the decision to invest in our solutions.

—Todd Harrison, director of leadership and associate development, WellPoint

The specific metric ROI is becoming less important, but that doesn't mean outcomes are unimportant—quite the opposite. However, we are finally recognizing that it is becoming increasingly difficult to measure ROI in a straightforward manner. Just twenty-five years ago, intangibles accounted for less than a third of the value of the S&P 500. Today, intangibles make up over 80 percent of the index value. For example, on paper (money paid for assets minus debt and depreciation), Google's net worth was $30 billion at the end of 2008. Yet, stock market investors valued Google at $125 billion. That extra $95 billion is intangibles.[81] We recognize the importance of such intangibles; in fact, CEOs reported that they would rather see business impact from learning over ROI.[82]

Professional development needs to be authentic and relative to the strategic needs of the business. It needs to occur in real time and be integrated with work that needs to be done. It also has to be aligned with how adults learn. Together, this means that it has to be adaptable to the individual, the team, and the business. Learning needs to adapt to changing business realities, cultures, customers, and clients. This requires: 1) awareness, 2) alignment, and 3) improvement. For learning to be real, engagement and collaboration are necessary.

—Kelli Price, senior vice president of people,
Premier, Inc.

Making the connection between learning and impact to business is what outcome-based learning is all about. That is not to say that continuous learning is a flawed model or that the genuine attempts to improve it are unwarranted. Continuous learning with a direct connection to application of that learning—what some call action learning—to a business issue is significantly better.

Having a problem you are trying to solve in mind can be a spark or catalyst that engages the person in their learning. It becomes a destination that they can work toward.

—Ruth Kennedy, director of organization
development, VF Corporation

Learn something to change something, to make something better, to improve something, as opposed to learning something because it just feels good to learn something is the difference between gaining knowledge and gaining wisdom. Wisdom is knowledge in action. Let's us not kid ourselves. There are many who enjoy the acquisition of knowledge for its own sake, and that's a wonderful thing—but that is not EPowerment. To take that knowledge and find ways to apply it and improve your condition or that of your organization is what EPowerment is all about.

The move from event-driven training to outcome-based permanent learning is forefront in our thinking. When we develop a leadership meeting or full training session, sustainability is included in the up-front design as opposed to being an afterthought. According to our internal research at Food Lion, LLC, when customers interact with another associate besides the cashier, their purchases increase by an average of 24 percent. We use that data point in training. The employees aren't just taught to ask, "Are you finding everything?" but also the reason behind that customer engagement, and that has had a huge benefit.

—Susan Richter, director of human resources,
Food Lion, LLC

Action learning (conceived by Reginald Revans, who concluded that conventional instructional methods were ineffective in the 1940s[83]) is an experience-based group learning process. People work in small groups and apply knowledge, theory, and concepts to solve real-world problems. During the action learning process, the work group develops a social culture of its own in which group members learn with and from each other.[84] Nearly all companies interviewed for this project cited action learning in use at their organizations in some form or another. The model helps employees not only reflect on what they have learned but process it and apply the newly acquired knowledge to their work.

We implement project-based learning. People come together and drive organizational priorities forward at the same time that they receive a learning experience. We have a development program for nominated senior directors and VPs that is based on action learning. Let's say there's potential for a new billion-dollar business. We divide people into grouped networks, and these group networks build a business plan. This creates competition between teams. The teams then present their solution to the board. The board selects a winner and the solution is implemented.

—Michelle Marquard, Fortune 100
Information Technology Company

Outcome-based learning is consistent with how we live our lives. For example, when you see the gas gauge in your car approaching empty, your immediate need is to get gas, and all your emotions and actions are driven toward getting gas so that you do not end up stranded. Your intended outcome is clear—to get gas. Getting gas then lets you do whatever else you need to do. Learning needs to be like this metaphor—it needs to answer the questions what purpose is the learning serving, what is the outcome, and how will you know if you have successfully achieved the outcome. Learning models that answer these questions truly create empowered workforces. And dare I say they would keep the CFO from cutting the development budget because the consequences would be clear? A less empowered workforce is the last thing we need, not only in challenging times but, especially, as we continue to navigate an environment of ever-increasing complexity.

OUTCOME-BASED LEARNING

Leader: Karie Willyerd, Sun Microsystems/Oracle
Karie Willyerd leads the award-winning Sun Learning Services (SLS) organization where she is responsible for employee, customer, partner, and community learning. Since joining Sun in 2005, Willyerd consolidated twelve disparate training and research-oriented functions at Sun into one cohesive group. She has spearheaded programs that make more learning available online—some in smaller packages of content and some at no charge. She has also driven a strategy to make learning accessible through different approach paths, such as by role, by product, by solution, and by certification path.

Company:
Sun Microsystems, Inc. provides network computing infrastructure solutions that include computer systems, software, storage, and services. Its core brands include the Java technology platform, the Solaris operating system, MySQL, StorageTek, and the UltraSPARC processor. Sun Microsystems is currently undergoing an acquisition by Oracle, combining best-in-class enterprise software and mission-critical computing systems.

Point of View:
Experience alone is not enough to learn how to be successful. Practice doesn't make perfect. Perfect practice makes perfect. In addition to gaining an experience, you must be thoughtful and reflective about the experiences you have. I am a constant learner. Any successful person who doesn't confess that luck has something to do with it isn't being as reflective as possible, either. So there is a little bit of luck as well.

OUTCOME-BASED LEARNING

Best Practices:
We have something we call the Leadership Connections program, which was co-created by the CEO. All executives of the company go through it. They meet with a coach, take assessments in advance, get feedback, and set learning goals prior to training.

Then at the end of the day, they make time for reflection moments. Everyone has a learning partner, and they go for a walk at the end of the day to discuss what they learned.

After two to four weeks, they meet with the coach again to reflect on what they learned. Then they have a toolkit that helps them pass on what they learned. Learning is not an event, it is a process—a process that plays out over time; it is not just the events you schedule. It takes people changing their brain chemistry over time to learn so you want to reinforce that learning through multiple streams and multiple time periods, this is the way to do it.

Goal Setting

People who set goals are tying their activities to an intended outcome. Simply stating an outcome increases the likelihood of achieving your vision, and the act of setting goals leads those who take the time to do so to be more successful than those who don't. A related item which complements goal-setting well, is that simply measuring something tends to produce an improvement. That's it, just measuring it, even without any explicit effort to improve. This is because we are often unaware of our actions. Simply keeping track of the calories you eat will result in you eating less, which will result in weight loss. In the office, simply filling out a status report daily or weekly will increase the amount of tangible things you get done. Now, imagine the results of not only setting some goals, but measuring them as well.

In the spirit of EPowerment, let's propose some changes to the traditional way of setting goals. Traditionally, we set a New Year's resolution on the first of January, work toward it for a few months, and then let it fizzle out and disappear (usually unachieved!) before spring rolls around. In the workplace, working professionals set goals once a year—whether it is formally or informally. They review these goals with their managers and then perhaps do a mid-year check on those goals.

While these haphazard methods may work some of the time, they tend to fail us most of the time. We make more excuses than we realize. We spend the lion's share of the performance review going over all the reasons why the goals were not met, and then, to top it off, we even put together a development plan that accommodates these excuses! When setting goals, consider incorporating SMART goals in order to buck this trend.

Continue to set annual goals, but use the popular SMART acronym to make sure the goals themselves are actually achievable. SMART refers to specific, measurable, actionable, realistic, and time-lined. There needs to be a non-debatable consensus on whether the goal was met or not—and that starts by setting the right goals. So what is a right goal? The right goal is related to concrete business needs. This is all the more important given that a recent study found that fewer than 5 percent of training programs are assessed in terms of their financial benefits to the organization.[85] Little wonder that training is one of the items to cut when budgets get tight.

Specific

Measurable

Actionable

Realistic

Timelined

Think of the year as a series of milestones and those milestones should be much more frequent than they are now. EPower your leaders to break annual goals into bite-sized chunks of months at a time—the cumulative sum of these milestones should match the annual goal. Then, leaders EPower their team to break the monthly goals into even smaller chunks of weekly activity that directly supports each goal. Finally, find a buddy (peer) or mentor or leverage technology for an external peer or mentor with whom you can share the monthly and weekly goals—this is similar to having a workout partner at the gym. Share your goals with each other and support each other's efforts to achieve them.

Consistently over-communicate your goals with your team. Having outcomes defined is one thing, having them bought into is quite another. This can only happen by engaging everyone who is a part of achieving that outcome. Some organizations and individuals actually post their goals in their e-mail signatures, through Tweets, on their Facebook pages, on their LinkedIn profiles, on their blogs, and through other social media platforms. Online status updates can be great for keeping you accountable— and you get support, encouragement, and sometimes even assistance from your network. The goals are visible for everyone and there has been great success in mutual support to achieving those goals.

There is a great story of a manager who wrote a blog about his recent performance review. He posted his annual goals for the world to see. Within a week, he had received hundreds of actionable ideas to help achieve them. He took those ideas back to the office and shared them with his entire staff, who then collectively divided those ideas into additional outcomes. They had their best quarter. This is EPowerment at work.

Having outcomes in mind is the best way to concretely map a journey. When you know where you want to go and can visualize the end in your mind, then it is easy to map a route to get there. If the route to the outcome is clear, then the learning required during the journey also becomes clear. In addition, the learning moments within that journey become more predictable. With this clarity, all the previous four principles to achieving EPowerment then have context.

The brevity of this chapter speaks to the simplicity of the concept. And to our credit, many of us set goals. The next step is to connect those goals to a learning strategy to achieve those goals. The more you know, the better your chances of achieving those goals. Success breeds success and confidence. This leads to higher EQ and greater empowerment, and again, it can best be achieved leveraging the new e world we all live in.

Summary and Key Points

- Outcome-based learning is not synonymous with continuous learning.
- Outcome-based learning is about connecting your newly acquired knowledge to a concrete outcome.
- Operationalize learning—make it relevant and measurable.
- There is not necessarily a positive relationship between liking the learning and a positive outcome. That takes a deliberate effort. By you.
- Action learning is outcome-based learning in a group setting where knowledge, theory, and concepts are applied to solve real-world problems.
- Connecting learning to business outcomes will please the CFO.
- Simply setting goals can help you succeed. Simply measuring something helps you improve.
- SMART goals are specific, measurable, actionable, realistic, and time-lined.
- Get buy-in and support for goals.

Chapter 10
Collective Human Knowledge

Use this book as a catalyst to "rethink" your paradigms. Consider your consumption habits, work habits, managerial habits, relationships, and the skills and abilities you bring to them. Seek new and better ways to do all that you do, especially in the context of getting yourselves and your employees to perform at much higher levels.

We must start by initiating a deep questioning of how things presently are. Do we do things at work because that's how they've always been done, or because that's how the competition does it, or because that's how the industry experts say we should do it? Are there better ways, cheaper, and more effective ways to get things done in the world of continued technology-enabled culture and workplace we live in?

For example, how much of your workforce really needs to come to a physical location every day? Why do people need offices? Why should there be forty-hour work weeks? Why are goals set annually and not quarterly or monthly? Why do we block people from using the Internet at work? Why do we have to wear a tie with a suit? Why shouldn't organizations be flat? Why shouldn't everyone get paid based on their performance? Why is collaborating with the competition a bad thing?

Why is bigger better? Why does cheaper mean lower value? How much time is really necessary to do your job? Why does everyone need a boss? Why shouldn't every employee own a P&L? Why are promotions and raises done annually? Why are commissions based on sales?

Perhaps you should consider getting rid of individual development plans (IDPs) or annual development plans, and consider a more positive and energizing term like EPowerment plans (EPs). Think about the psychological difference between working on an IDP versus an EP? Imagine yourself as a leader saying to your staff, "Let's work on your EPpowerment plan" as opposed to the dreaded "Let's work on your development plan." Which one do you thing is emotionally enabling? Which gives a sense of renting? Owning?

This book presents a powerful case for just how dramatic a change in how we live and work we have been through, are going through, and will continue to go through. The list of technology accessories alone that we possess today, juxtaposed to twenty years ago, is unprecedented, and likely to double in half the time moving forward. We discussed the impact of the 2008 – 2009 recession, the changing demographics of the workforce, technology, and globalization. Times are changing.

This book reviewed in detail why empowerment has never been more achievable and necessary than today. And to achieve this state, personally, and organizationally, we have to leverage the new art and science of emotional intelligence to complement our skills and competencies in the e world. The book argues that this combination will lead to realizing greater potential and taking advantage of the inherent opportunities in the major forces of change already discussed. Previous chapters presented a set of principles supported by case studies, research, and anecdotal evidence from practitioners and thought leaders from a myriad of organizations from all over the world. Clearly, there is consensus in what we have shared with you.

Part of the magic of empowerment is the ability to capture more *aha!* moments as they naturally occur in life and the workplace. The five principles are a sound model to do just that:

1. **Extended Learning Models:** Forget about learning as an event that occurs when it is scheduled somewhere by someone. The opportunity to learn occurs when we are ready to learn whenever that is, which can only come through an extended learning model.

2. **Emotional Safety:** Substantive learning happens in an emotionally safe environment. Think about how you are creating that emotionally safe place for collaboration and innovation.

3. **Multiple Modalities:** One size has never fit all. It was a model that existed because there simply weren't better ones out there. Effective learning that leads to empowerment occurs in the modality preferred by the individual learner. Thus, multi-mode learning is needed, and it has never before been more available.

4. **Mentoring:** There is simply no substitute for a mentor. Mentoring is the most tried-and-true model we have had for learning and empowerment. Empowerment is maximized when it comes from a mentor—someone who can be objective and has context for your life.

5. **Outcomes:** When you acquire new knowledge specifically for an immediate need that requires the application of the knowledge, you maximize your EPower. Teachers, trainers, coaches, and learners all must ask, "How can I apply this to what I do to make better decisions?"

Is it a stretch to imagine that your organization can be in a daily state of learning and subsequent empowerment? What would your organization be like if this were true? Designing an organization's performance around these five principles will best set you and your workforce up for harnessing collective human knowledge and reaching the optimal human potential. This is EPowerment. Are you EPowered?

We want to conclude this book by harnessing the collective wisdom of human capital professionals from all over the world, from all industries, who have committed their professional lives to EPowering themselves and their organizations. This is their wisdom, offered for you to consider as you move into the next decade:

Jeannene H. Allen, human resource director, CVS Caremark / CVS Pharmacy

- The million dollar question for any leader is, "Did you leave the organization in a better place than when you found it?"
- Be passionate about what you do. If you aren't passionate about your job and career, there is a line of people standing behind you who would love to have your job.

- Focus on your values and vision for your life by setting long-term, short-term, and daily goals. Take time to have fun each day. Reflect on your achievements and shortfalls, otherwise life is just a blur of events.

Richard Bergeron, manager of talent development, Goodyear
- It's okay to take a chance. If you win, celebrate with your team. If you don't win, learn from your mistake so you won't repeat it.
- If you're going to be an instigator of any performance change process, get to know the people you work with and the culture of your organization first.

Bill Bonstetter, CEO, and Ashley Bowers, president, TTI
- Identify the key accountabilities for all jobs that impact the bottom line and determine the skills, behavior, reward system, and emotional intelligence required for superior performance.
- Make sure to involve as many employees as possible in the decision-making process so they feel valued and a real part of the company.
- Use metrics to measure the return on investment (ROI) on people solutions to prove the ROI of job matching, training, etc.
- Make sure all your performance management systems for employee development are job-related.

Jerry Conway, VP of human resources, Domtar
- Focus on results rather than activities or mandated processes. Give people a tool set to get the desired

results, and be clear relative to expectations and support mechanisms.

- Implement stretch assignments for people who have fire in their belly—the perfect hire or promotion is a myth anyway. People will grow through challenging work. You can train a person to do a lot of things, but passion, honesty, and courage are not on that list.
- Breakthrough leadership is a function of also being a good follower. Educate present and future leaders about the synergies of informed alignment.

Patricia Crull, CLO, Time Warner Cable
- Know that you are responsible for your world—at home, at work, in your community—so make it better every day by taking care of the duties closest to you. Ask yourself frequently, "What can I do right now to make this situation more constructive?"
- Give generously to others. Give information, recognition, praise, feedback, and support. It will help you to recognize and savor all that has been generously given to you.
- Grow spiritually, emotionally, mentally, and physically, so that, at the end of your career, all aspects of you are as vital as the day you began your life's work.

Vincent Davis, general manager – development, quality, and business support, Duke Energy
- As technology continues to facilitate our ability to move faster, make sure to take a moment of pause before making critical decisions.

- Always remember that the truth is the best answer. The urge to not disclose mistakes in fear of a negative reaction must be overcome by the courage it takes to do the right thing.
- Effective leaders must assess who they need to be for the team to be successful at each given moment. Leadership is not always about being in command and control. It is also about being in tune with what the organization needs from you in order for the organization to be successful. Those needs can and will change, and your leadership style should embrace this change.

Suzy Domenick Burnham, vice president of human resources, Prudential

- Understand and appreciate the differences in the people you lead and with whom you work. Bring together those differences so that you can create the best outcome for all.
- Surround yourself with great people; people who are smarter than you, more creative than you, and who balance your style. Never be afraid or intimidated by those who are better or more creative, but instead be appreciative of what they will ultimately do for the company and for you.
- Create an environment of open communication, share your knowledge, praise publicly, and ensure your team provides feedback to you continuously. Strive to always be a better leader.

Ana Dutra, CEO, leadership and talent consulting, Korn/Ferry International

- Focus on giving more than taking, focus on developing others as a means to develop yourself, focus on enabling rather than taking over, focus on learning rather than teaching—that's when real leadership is created.
- Prioritize, prioritize, prioritize around your main life purpose: the risk of operating in an ultra-connected world is exactly to get lost in so many possibilities and connections.
- Do not underestimate the power of a face-to-face interaction, the power of undivided attention, and deep, long lasting friendships. Nurture and enjoy a few deep relationships throughout your life.

Troy Heflin, VP of organizational development, Volvo

- Have the courage to increase your self-awareness. The most significant professional development occurs when we become newly aware of a limiting issue, when we are able to make a connection from our past to it, and when we can see how loudly it now stands in the way of our future direction.
- Be the leader you want to follow. As a leader, model behavior you expect from others. As a follower, learn from both good and bad leaders.
- If you are willing to apply yourself, you can go in any direction. You are in charge of your own career.

Steve Eller, vice president of human resources at Robert Bosch, LLC

- Speak with data and facts. Don't make the conversation personal.
- Know your surroundings. Learn from your mistakes and the mistakes of others.
- Maintain the proper balance. Work may be your career, but your family is your life.

Anne Feller, organizational development, Cox Communications
- Engage people's hearts and create communities. Otherwise, you'll have people renting jobs rather than owning jobs.
- Make the workplace more like family. Engage the boomers with Gen X and Gen Y so you have that sense of family that will become more and more important.
- If we want the customer to experience good feelings with us, we need to experience those same feelings within.

Michelle A. Fish, entrepreneur, founder and CEO, Integra (Inc. Fastest Growing Company and Best Places to Work)
- Entrepreneurs do not have all the resources as established companies. We *rely* on empowered associates, so EPower is a great model for us.
- Entrepreneurial companies will also rely heavily on contract work and performance-based work. It is thus to our advantage to create the workplace that allows all kinds of diverse employees to perform their best.
- Successful entrepreneurs should view their workforce as mosaic of people and skills from anywhere in the

world. It is cheaper, more effective, and less stressful than carrying huge overheads.

Brian Formato, global director, organizational leadership and development, Doosan

- A critical characteristic for success in the future will be personal agility. Agility encompasses the concept of change readiness with speed. In the past, being open to new ideas and willing to change was enough. In the future, the speed with which individuals anticipate and adapt to change will be a major differentiator of those who excel and those who just survive.
- It used to be that people who enjoyed working with computers and technology were geeks. Today, and, more importantly, in the future being tech savvy will be a requirement. Leaders need to understand the technologies available to them both in the form of smart phones and desktop applications. These efficiency tools can be game changers. Those who embrace technology and learn to leverage technology to their personal advantage will come out the winners.
- The investor mentality. As a leader, be an investor. Focus on increasing your market value by constantly providing additional value. When making career choices, think of each job as an investment in your future potential.

Debra Gmelin, corporate director, leadership institute, Humana

- Creating and sustaining relationships is the most important capability for those who wish to have a long, successful career.
- Look back at your past successes and failures, but don't stare. Create positive momentum forward through continuous self-awareness.
- Be willing to develop and inspire others. Lighting one's candle doesn't diminish your own fire.

Nolan Godfrey, organizational development, Boehringer-Ingelheim

- Have perfect integrity. This means doing what you say you'll do and what you believe in your heart to be right. Integrity is the cornerstone of trust. If you have integrity, you will be trusted. This is so much needed in our days, given that we are increasingly persuaded to accept or follow leaders of questionable integrity.
- Work toward total engagement. The leader or organization that can treat people in a way that they voluntarily bring their whole selves to their work will have an enormous advantage. People need and have always needed to be appreciated, understood, and encouraged to contribute in meaningful ways. This will become increasingly important as the machinations of modern markets churn across the globe.
- Create the future. Sometimes we plan based on how the world changes around us. Why not instead change ourselves and the world around us, and make that our plan? Lead out in bold and courageous endeavors to improve the human experience instead of waiting for another to dictate it to you.

Todd Harrison, director of leadership and associate development, WellPoint

- Be decisive! Be capable of making sound, independent decisions when necessary.
- Be focused on talent management from an individualized perspective. Tap into people's unique motivations.
- Be visible. With the significant advent of a more virtual workplace in many companies over the past decade, the need to over-communicate is even more important, especially in tough times.
- Change how human capital managers work; transition from the industrial-age mentality to the one of the knowledge age. Knowledge can be found anywhere. Once we in the human capital industry are comfortable with that, only then can we leverage that for the betterment of our organizations.

Effenus Henderson, chief diversity officer, Weyerhaeuser

- Be bold, not ordinary. Think creatively about the future.
- Be inclusive. Seek to draw out perspectives that may not come out otherwise.
- Be humble in how you do business. Have a lifelong learning orientation. Learning brings awareness and awareness raises your own shortcomings.
- Develop your mental agility. Improve not only your ability to quickly get the big picture, but your ability to take that strategic viewpoint from the 50,000-foot view down to the details. Understand how the elements within the system influence each other.

Most people are good at either the big picture or the detailed thinking, but it is a rare and agile leader that can do both.

Kevin Henry, chief HR officer, Coca-Cola Bottling
- Lead with humility, lead with conviction, lead with courage.
- Lead with a servant's heart, putting the interests of those you lead above and in front your own.
- Never underestimate the power of the individual, and, when that effect is multiplied by several thousand, how impactful that can be on an organization. Investing in human capital by helping people realize their full potential has got to be a priority.
- Be prepared to deal with two types of change. One is change that you must react to; the other type is the change that you will lead.

Bill Hodgetts, VP of corporate leadership development, Fidelity
- So much more is possible than what we have done today. Don't be limited by current assumptions of relationships that have been created by existing frameworks and organizations.
- Bring more love and caring into the world through your work.
- Be appreciative of the benefits positive psychology can bring to talent management, leadership development, and human capital. A lot of good lessons can be mined from this field.

Ann Johnson, director of management development, Mattel

- Drive for results.
- Develop your people.
- Leave a legacy.

Ruth Kennedy, director of organization development, VF Corporation
- Know who you are; including your beliefs and assumptions, functional competencies, and leadership competencies. Know who you are as a leader, what makes up your base, and how you can leverage that.
- Be a student of yourself and others, starting today. You can't know it all and you can't be it all. Learn how to pull the potential of others to bring depths to projects. Learn to leverage people. It's not about you but the people who are following you and helping you.
- "I can do it myself" is the worst mode for a leader to be in. "It's not a single thread that makes the fabric; it is multiple threads that make up the pattern."

Leticia Knowles, diversity and inclusion, American Express
- Become comfortable dealing with conflict. When a manager is uncomfortable with conflict, he or she cannot carry out his or her duties properly and allows issues to go unaddressed.

Steve Larson, senior VP of diversity, engagement, and inclusion, Wells Fargo
- Listen to front line employees' experiences. This is where a lot of learning and awareness comes from.

- Learn about other cultures. A lack of awareness of others' culture is the core of most conflicts because the expectations are different. Understand how your cultural norms match up with others' cultural norms, and prepare behavioral strategies to deal with that.

Jane Luciano, VP of global learning and organizational development, Bristol-Myers Squibb

- Find your own niche, and be comfortable with that niche. For example, I know I don't have all the answers. The best thing I contribute is a great question that can take thinking further. It took a while, but I am comfortable that that is what I bring to the party.
- As the world changes, as there is more competition for talent globally, *you* as the talent have to rise to the top of the war for talent. Be sought after. Today, there is a pressure to keep your skill set sharp and pressure to take care of your own performance, so bring the best skill set to the table.
- You spend a lot of time giving and doing. If you are passionate about what you are giving and doing, you will do your best work.
- Ensure that people are better because you have touched them. Servant leadership pays you back one-hundred-fold.

Emma Oberdieck, people development, YUM! Brands, Inc.

- Be flexible. The needs of our world and our employers are constantly changing. Being willing to take on the new assignment or to make the lateral move will keep your skills fresh and keep you in demand.

- Seek knowledge. We are training today for jobs that will be obsolete in the not-too-distant future. Rather than saying "I know it all," say "What can I learn now?"
- Build relationships. People like to work with people they like and trust. Reaching out to know someone better will strengthen your relationship and will allow you to make the big requests of each other when necessary.

Linda Palumbo, talent solutions, 3M
- Be flexible and creative. Don't get stuck in bureaucracy or give up too quickly. Look for ways to overcome obstacles when you encounter them.
- Take some risks, bend the rules a bit, and do the right thing.
- Be a lifelong learner. You must continue to learn to stay current and relevant.
- Be real. Admitting that you make mistakes and sharing what you learn from them will earn you respect and encourage others to be innovative and take risks.

Kelli Price, senior vice president of people, Premier, Inc.
- Organizations must be authentic and real. To get that, we must have real and authentic leaders.
- Leaders must align all people around a common purpose that inspires them to best performance. Great leaders must empower people to step out and lead in a way that highly motivates and engages all people across an organization to be and give their best to fulfill the collective purpose.

- It is all about empowering employees, customers, and organizations. EQ is needed for a leader to model that effectively.
- People and workforce practices should align with expected business strategies and drive high-performance work and people engagement.

Susan Richter, director of human resources, Food Lion, LLC
- Listen more than you talk.
- Don't think you have all the answers.
- Practice reflection often. If you hear something that is completely against your current thinking, strive to understand that person's thinking and consider how you might use that in your world.

Stan Sword, VP total rewards, Sprint/Nextel
- Understand what you are uniquely gifted to do, and apply yourself to a cause or business that you are passionate about.
- Make emerging technologies work for you versus having them "run" your life.
- Focus on meaningful relationships and the things that really make a difference.

Karie Willyerd, chief learning officer, Sun Microsystems
- Learn how to have a more democratic leadership style (I call it "Citizen Leader" in my book, *The 2020 Workforce*). Be open to getting lots and lots of feedback—genuinely solicit it and look forward to hearing it.

- Leadership is about followership. There is no such thing as a leader without followers.
- A great leader in one situation might not survive in another situation.
- As a leader, be the first among equals rather than having all the answers and solutions and everyone else get behind you.

Eric Wiseman, chairman, president, and CEO of VF Corporation

- Leaders need to communicate in a way that inspires. They need to inspire teamwork, performance, trust, integrity, and confidence, and they need to do this consistently, every single day.
- VF is a team sport. We don't use the word "I" around here much. It's a "we" driven culture that creates powerful internal partnerships that win and lose together. We're very protective of this piece of our culture.
- People need to be comfortable sharing information, good or bad. They need to be brutally honest.

Linda Worden, director of training and organizational development, MeadWestvaco Corporation:

- Leaders need to understand that the value they add is not what unique information and knowledge they hold but the ability to leverage collaborative relationships. The value-add of the leader of the next decade is changing from "individual contributor" to "leveraging collaborative relationships."

- Second, future leaders should be out there, familiarizing themselves with different people, different cultures, and different things and putting priority on becoming lifelong learners.

Bob Zierk, VP of human resources, Black & Decker:
- Develop your soft skills to achieve positions of greater responsibility.
- Be willing to give away and delegate authority. In doing this, you are not giving any of your power or responsibility away; instead, you are driving accountability and decision making at the lower levels of the organization.
- Create a balance between seriousness and fun, in a relaxed atmosphere, so people like to come to work and can be engaged in their work.
- Change will come, so stay current with technology. Embrace the change because change presents an opportunity.
- Be willing to take risks and fail—but learn from it. It increases your self-awareness and in turn, makes you a better performer and leader.

Endnotes

Chapter 1

1. Mercer, "Human capital planning 2010: Resetting the talent and rewards agenda," (2009): http://www.mercer. com/attachment.dyn?idContent=1356290&filePath=/ attachments/English/HCP2010_POV_final.pdf.
2. Chris Argyris, "Empowerment: The emperor's new clothes," *Harvard Business Review* (1998): 98.
3. Peter Kizilos, "Crazy about empowerment?" *Training* 27, no. 12 (1990), 47.
4. Aon Consulting, "Benefits and talent survey," (2008): http:// www.aon.mediaroom.com/.
5. Randstad, "Tenth annual world of work survey," (2009): http://www.us.randstad.com/.
6. Stephen Gandel, "Why boomers can't quit," *Time*. (2009): http://www.time.com/time/specials/packages/ article/0,28804,1898024_1898023_1898080,00.html.
7. Jack Van Derhei, "The impact of the recent financial crisis

on 401(k) account balances," *EBRI Issue Brief,* no. 326 (2009): http://www.ebri.org/pdf/briefspdf/EBRI_IB_2-2009_Crisis-Impct.pdf.

8. Ruth Helman, Craig Copeland, and Jack VanDerhei, "The 2009 retirement confidence survey: Economy drives confidence to record lows; many looking to work longer," *EBRI Issue Brief,* no. 328 (2009): http://www.ebri.org/pdf/briefspdf/EBRI_IB_4-2009_RCS2.pdf.

9. Gandel, "Why boomers can't quit," *Time.*

10. Kelly Greene, "Baby boomers delay retirement," *The Wall Street Journal* (2008): http://online.wsj.com/article/SB122204345024061453.html.

11. United States Department of Labor, "Current unemployment rates for states and historical highs/lows," *Bureau of Labor Statistics* (2009): http://stats.bls.gov/web/lauhsthl.htm.

12. Robert Gavin, "Losing jobs in unequal numbers," *The Boston Globe* (December 5, 2008): A-1, A-8.

13. National Association of Colleges and Employers, "2009 student survey," (2009): http://www.naceweb.org/Research/Student/Student_Survey.aspx.

14. Sylvia Ann Hewlett, Laura Sherbin, and Karen Sumberg, "How Gen Y and boomers will reshape your agenda," *Harvard Business Review,* (2009): 71.

15. United States Department of Labor, "Number of jobs held, labor market activity, and earnings growth among the youngest baby boomers: Results from a longitudinal survey," *Bureau of Labor Statistics* (2008): http://www.bls.gov/news.release/nlsoy.toc.htm.

16. Ulric Neisser, "Rising scores on intelligence tests," *American Scientist* 85, (1997): 440.

17. Daniel Goleman, "Are women more emotionally intelligent than men?" *The Huffington Post* (posted June 4, 2009): http://www.huffingtonpost.com/dan-goleman/are-women-more-emotionall_b_211591.html.

18. Claire Shipman and Katty Kay, "Women will rule business," *Time* (2009): http://www.time.com/time/specials/packages/article/0,28804,1898024_1898023_1898078,00.html.

19. Catalyst, "The bottom line: Connecting corporate performance and gender diversity," (2004): http://www.catalyst.org/publication/82/the-bottom-line-connecting-corporate-performance-and-gender-diversity.

20. Michelle Conlin, "Smashing the clock," *Business Week* (2006): http://www.businessweek.com/magazine/content/06_50/b4013001.htm.

21. Michelle Conlin, "Gap to employees: Work wherever, whenever you want," *Business Week* (2009): http://www.businessweek.com/careers/managementiq/archives/2009/09/gap_to_employee.html.

22. United States Department of Labor, "Employment projections: 2008-18," *Bureau of Labor Statistics* (2009): http://www.bls.gov/news.release/pdf/ecopro.pdf.

23. Jagdish Bhagwati and Alan S. Blinder, *Offshoring of American jobs: What response from U.S. economic policy?* (The MIT Press, 2009), 1-144.

24. Thomas Jackson, Ray Dawson, and Darren Wilson, "The cost of e-mail interruption," *Journal of Systems and Information Technology 5* (2001): 81.

25. Watson Wyatt, "WorkUSA 2006/2007: Debunking the myths of employee engagement," (2007): http://www.watsonwyatt.com/research/resrender.asp?id=2006-US-0039&page=1.

Chapter 2

26. Jennifer Ballard, "Huge global growth in SMS continues over the new year period," *Acision* (2008): http://www.acision. com/media_detail.aspx?id_menu=media&id_sub=Press%20 Releases&id_rd=Huge%20global%20growth%20in%20 SMS%20continues%20over%20the%20new%20year%20 period.

27. Wakefield Research, "In-flight Wi-Fi takes off: Frequent flyers, business travelers say it tops other airline amenities," *Wi-Fi Alliance* (2009): http://www.wi-fi.org/news_articles. php?f=media_news&news_id=847.

28. Andrew Lipsman, "61 billion searches conducted worldwide in August," *comScore* (2007): http://www.comscore.com/ Press_Events/Press_Releases/2007/10/Worldwide_Searches_ Reach_61_Billion.

29. Robert Roche, "The Wireless Association announces semi-annual wireless industry survey results," *CTIA* (2009): http:// www.businesswire.com/news/google/20091007006200/en/ CTIA%E2%80%93The-Wireless-Association-Announces-Semi-Annual-Wireless-Industry.

30. Karl Fisch, Scott McLeod, and Jeff Brenman, "Did you know?" (2008): http://www.youtube.com/watch?v=cL9Wu2 kWwSY&feature=player_embedded.

31. Paul Hemp, "Death by information overload: New research and novel techniques offer a lifeline to you and your organization," *Harvard Business Review* (2009): 89.

32. Bree Nordenson, "Overload! Journalism's battle for relevance in an age of too much information," *Columbia Journalism Review* (2008): http://www.cjr.org/feature/overload_1.php.

33. Thomas L. Friedman, *The World Is Flat 3.0: A Brief History of The Twenty-First Century* (New York: Picador, 2007).

34. Roberts Jones, Kathryn Scanland, and Steve Gunderson, *The jobs revolution: Changing how America works* (Copywriters, Inc., 2004).

35. Fisch, et al., "Did you know?"

36. U.S. Department of Labor, "Number of jobs, labor market experience, and earnings growth."

37. U.S. Department of Labor, "Employee tenure in 2008," *Bureau of Labor Statistics* (2008): http://www.bls.gov/news.release/tenure.htm.

38. Marc Prensky, "Digital natives, digital immigrants," *On the Horizon* 9 no. 5 (2001).

39. Sun Microsystems, "Open work: Overview," (2009): http://www.sun.com/aboutsun/openwork/index.jsp.

40. Ryan M. Johnson, "Telework trendlines 2009," *WorldatWork* (2009): http://www.workingfromanywhere.org/news/Trendlines_2009.pdf.

41. Michael O'Brien, "Long-distance relationship troubles," *HR Executive* (2009): http://www.hrexecutive.com/HRE/story.jsp?storyId=229836658.

42. Matthew Glotzbach, "Ten things you couldn't do last year," Presented at the Office 2.0 Conference, 2008.

Chapter 3

43. Andrew Campbell, Jo Whitehead, and Syndey Finkelstein, "Why good leaders make bad decisions," *Harvard Business Review* (2009).

44. John Gottman, *Why marriages succeed or fail: And how you*

can make yours last (New York: Simon & Schuster, Inc., 1995).
45

Chapter 4

45. Lilian Hayes Martin, *The business devotional* (Sterling Innovation 2009), 181.

46. Ranstad, "Tenth annual world of work survey."

47. W. Edwards Deming, *Out of the crisis: Quality, productivity, and competitive position* (Cambridge: Cambridge University Press, 1986).

Chapter 5

48. Kenneth Wexley and Gary Latham, *Developing and training human resources in organizations (3rd ed.)* (Upper Saddle River, NJ: Prentice Hall, 2002).

49. Louis Augustus Pechstein, "Massed vs. distributed effort in learning," *Journal of Educational Psychology*, 12, no. 2 (1921): 92-97.

50. Helene M. Sisti, Arnold L. Glass, and Tracey J. Shors, "Neurogenesis and the spacing effect: Learning over time enhances memory and the survival of new neurons," *Learning and Memory* (2007).

51. Clinton O. Longenecker and Laurence S. Fink, "Management training: Benefits and lost opportunities (part II)," *Industrial and Commercial Training* 37, no 2. (2005): 73-79.

52. Longenecker, "Management training."

53. Dobbin Frank, Alexandra Kalev and Erin Kelly, "Diversity management in corporate America: Do America's costly

diversity management programs work? Not always," *Contexts* 6, no 4 (2007): 21-27.

54. Committee on Quality of Health Care in America, and Institute of Medicine, *To err Is human: Building a safer health system.* ed. Linda T. Kohn, Janet M. Corrigan, and Molla S. Donaldson (Washington, DC: National Academy Press, 1999).

Chapter 6

55. Hayes, *The business devotional,* 62.

56. Lymari Morales, "Self-employed workers clock the most hours each week," *Gallup* (2009): http://www.gallup.com/poll/122510/Self-Employed-Workers-Clock-Hours-Week.aspx.

57. Pascal Thibault, Patrick Bourgeois, and Usrula Hess, "The effect of group-identification on emotion recognition: The case of cats and basketball players," *Journal of Experimental Social Psychology,* 42 (2006): 676-683.

58. Ranstad, "Tenth annual world of work survey."

59. Watson Wyatt, "WorkUSA 2006/2007."

60. Alicia Grandey, "Emotion regulation in the workplace: A new way to conceptualize emotional labor," *Journal of Occupational Health Psychology,* 5 (2000): 59-100.

61. Anat Rafaeli and Robert Sutton, "Expression of emotion as part of the work role," *Academy of Management Review,* 12 (1987): 23-37.

62. Alicia Grandey, "When 'the show must go on': Surface acting and deep acting as determinants of emotional exhaustion and peer-rated service delivery," *Academy of Management Journal,* 46 (2003): 86-96.

63. Benedict Carey, "Fear in the workplace: The bullying boss," *New York Times,* (2004): http://www.nytimes. com/2004/06/22/health/fear-in-the-workplace-the-bullying-boss.html.

64. EQmentor, http://www.eqmentor.com.

Chapter 7

65. Diane Coutu and Carol Kauffman, "What can coaches do for you?" *Harvard Business Review,* (2009).

66. Alta Mesa Group, "The establishment of executive coaching: 2007 trends in executive expectations and performance management," (2007): http://www.pearsonpartnersintl.com/pdfs/AM_ExecutiveCoaching.pdf.

67. Hewlett, et al., "How Gen Y and boomers will reshape your agenda."

Chapter 8

68. Roland H. Andrews, "The development of a learning styles program in a low socioeconomic, underachieving North Carolina elementary school," *Journal of Reading, Writing, and Learning Disabilities: International* 6, no. 3 (1990): 307-314.

69. Robert O. Neely and Duane Alm, "Meeting individual needs: A learning styles success story," *Clearing House* 66, no. 2 (1992): 109-113.

70. Eric Rodgers, "Executing blended learning," *Chief Learning Officer* (2009).

71. Erica Gordon Sorohan, "We do; therefore we learn," *Training and Development* 4, no. 10 (1993): 47-55.

72. Mary Madden, "The audience for online video-sharing sites

shoots up," *Pew Internet* (2009): http://fe01.pewinternet.org/ Reports/2009/13--The-Audience-for-Online-VideoSharing-Sites-Shoots-Up.aspx.

73. Jim Giles, "Special Report: Internet encyclopaedias go head to head," *Nature 438*(2005): 900-901.

74. Sharon Gaudin, "Study: 54 percent of companies ban Facebook, Twitter at work," *Computer World* (2009): http:// www.computerworld.com/s/article/9139020/Study_54_of_ companies_ban_Facebook_Twitter_at_work.

75. Brent Coker, "Freedom to surf: Workers more productive if allowed to use the Internet for leisure," *University of Melbourne* (2009): http://uninews.unimelb.edu.au/news/5750/.

76. Coker, "Freedom to surf."

77. Hayden Shaw, "Modular series: Leading across generations," *Franklin Covey.*

Chapter 9

78. Lucy Kellaway, "The year of the CFO," *The Economist* (2009): http://www.economist.com/theworldin/displayStory. cfm?story_id=12494665&d=2009.

79. Kevin Hook and David Bunce, "Immediate learning in organizational computer training as a function of training intervention affective reaction and session impact measures," *Applied Psychology* 50, no. 3 (2001): 436-454.

80. Sitzmann, et al., "A review and meta-analysis of the nomological network of trainee reactions," *Journal of Applied Psychology* 93, no. 2 (2008): 280-295.

81. Thomas Stewart, *The wealth of knowledge: Intellectual capital and the twenty-first century organization* (Doubleday, 2001).

82. Jack Phillips and Patti Phillips, "The real reason we don't evaluate," *Chief Learning Officer* (2009).

83. Reginald Revans, *Action learning: New techniques for management* (London: Blond & Briggs, Ltd., 1980); Reginald Revans, *The origin and growth of action learning* (Brickley, UK: Chartwell-Bratt., 1982); Reginald Revans, *ABC of action learning* (London: Lemos and Crane., 1988).

84. Joseph A. Raelin, "Action learning and action science: Are they different?" *Organizational Dynamics*, 26 (1997): 21-34.

85. Richard A. Swanson, *Assessing the financial benefits of human resource development* (Cambridge, MA: Perseus, 2001).

Bibliography

Alta Mesa Group. "The establishment of executive coaching: 2007 trends in executive expectations and performance management." (2007): http://www.pearsonpartnersintl.com/pdfs/AM_ExecutiveCoaching.pdf.

Andrews, Roland H. "The development of a learning styles program in a low socioeconomic, underachieving North Carolina elementary school." *Journal of Reading, Writing, and Learning Disabilities: International* 6, no. 3 (1990): 307-314.

Aon Consulting. "Benefits and talent survey." (2008): http://www.aon.mediaroom .com/.

Argyris, Chris. "Empowerment: The emperor's new clothes." *Harvard Business Review* (1998): 98-105.

Ballard, Jennifer. "Huge global growth in SMS continues over the new year period." *Acision* (2008): http://www.acision.com/media_detail.aspx?id_menu=media&id_sub=Press%20Releases&id_rd=Huge%20global%20growth%20in%20SMS%20continues%20over%20the%20new%20year%20period.

Bhagwati, Jagdish, and Alan S. Blinder, *Offshoring of American jobs: What response from U.S. economic policy?* The MIT Press, 2009.

Campbell, Andrew, Jo Whitehead, and Syndey Finkelstein. "Why good leaders make bad decisions." *Harvard Business Review* (2009).

Carey, Benedict. "Fear in the workplace: The bullying boss." *New York Times,* (2004): http://www.nytimes.com/2004/06/22/health/fear-in-the-workplace-the-bullying-boss.html.

Catalyst. "The bottom line: Connecting corporate performance and gender diversity." (2004): http://www.catalyst.org/publication/82/the-bottom-line-connecting-corporate-performance-and-gender-diversity.

Coker, Brent. "Freedom to surf: Workers more productive if allowed to use the internet for leisure." *University of Melbourne* (2009): http://uninews.unimelb.edu.au/news/5750/.

Committee on Quality of Health Care in America, and Institute of Medicine, *To err Is human: Building a safer health system.* Edited by Linda T. Kohn, Janet M. Corrigan, and Molla S. Donaldson. Washington, D.C.: National Academy Press, 1999.

Conlin, Michelle "Smashing the clock." *Business Week* (2006): http://www.businessweek.com/magazine/content/06_50/b4013001.htm.

———. "Gap to employees: Work wherever, whenever you want." *Business Week* (2009): http://www.businessweek.com/careers/managementiq/archives/2009/09/gap_to_employee.html.

Coutu, Diane and Carol Kauffman. "What can coaches do for you?" *Harvard Business Review,* (2009).

Deming, W. Edwards. *Out of the crisis: Quality, productivity, and competitive position.* Cambridge: Cambridge University Press, 1986.

Fisch, Karl, Scott McLeod, and Jeff Brenman. "Did you know?" (2008): http://www.youtube.com/watch?v=cL9Wu2kWwSY &feature=player_embedded.

Frank, Dobbin, Alexandra Kalev, and Erin Kelly. "Diversity management in Corporate America: Do America's costly diversity management programs work? Not always." *Contexts* 6, no 4 (2007): 21-27.

Friedman, Thomas L. *The World Is Flat 3.0: A Brief History of The Twenty-First Century.* New York: Picador, 2007.

Gandel, Stephen. "Why boomers can't quit." *Time.* (2009): http://www.time.com/time/specials/packages/article/0,28804,1898024_1898023_1898080,00.html.

Gaudin, Sharon. "Study: 54 percent of companies ban Facebook, Twitter at work." *Computer World* (2009): http://www.computerworld.com/s/article/9139020/Study_54_of_companies_ban_Facebook_Twitter_at_work.

Gavin, Robert. "Losing jobs in unequal numbers." *The Boston Globe* (December 5, 2008): A-1, A-8.

Jim Giles, "Special Report: Internet encyclopaedias go head to head," *Nature 438*(2005): 900-901.

Glotzbach, Matthew. "Ten things you couldn't do last year." Presented at the Office 2.0 Conference, 2008.

Goleman, Daniel. "Are women more emotionally intelligent than men?" *The Huffington Post* (posted June 4, 2009): http://www.huffingtonpost.com/dan-goleman/are-women-more-emotionall_b_211591.html.

Gottman, John. *Why marriages succeed or fail: And how you can make yours last.* New York: Simon & Schuster, Inc., 1995.

Grandey, Alicia. "Emotion regulation in the workplace: A new way to conceptualize emotional labor." *Journal of Occupational Health Psychology,* 5 (2000): 59-100.

————. "When 'the show must go on': Surface acting and deep acting as determinants of emotional exhaustion and peer-rated service delivery." *Academy of Management Journal,* 46 (2003): 86-96.

Greene, Kelly. "Baby boomers delay retirement." *The Wall Street Journal* (2008): http://online.wsj.com/article/SB122204345024061453.html.

Helman, Ruth, Craig Copeland, and Jack Van Derhei. "The 2009 retirement confidence survey: Economy drives confidence to record lows; many looking to work longer." *EBRI Issue Brief,* no. 328 (2009): http://www.ebri.org/pdf/briefspdf/EBRI_IB_4-2009_RCS2.pdf.

Hemp, Paul. "Death by information overload: New research and novel techniques offer a lifeline to you and your organization." *Harvard Business Review* (2009): 82-89.

Hewlett, Sylvia Ann, Laura Sherbin, and Karen Sumberg. "How Gen Y and Boomers will reshape your agenda." *Harvard Business Review,* (2009): 71-76.

Hook, Kevin, and David Bunce. "Immediate learning in organizational computer training as a function of training intervention affective reaction and session impact measures." *Applied Psychology* 50, no. 3 (2001): 436-454.

Jackson, Thomas, Ray Dawson, and Darren Wilson. "The cost

of e-mail interruption." *Journal of Systems and Information Technology* 5 (2001): 81-92.

Johnson, Ryan M. "Telework trendlines 2009." *WorldatWork* (2009): http://www.workingfromanywhere.org/news/Trendlines_2009.pdf.

Jones, Roberts, Kathryn Scanland, and Steve Gunderson. *The jobs revolution: Changing how America works.* Copywriters, Inc., 2000.

Kellaway, Lucy. "The year of the CFO." *The Economist* (2009): http://www.economist.com/theworldin/displayStory.cfm?story_id=12494665&d=2009.

Kizilos, Peter. "Crazy about empowerment?" *Training* 27, no. 12 (1990): 47-53.

Lipsman, Andrew. "61 billion searches conducted worldwide in August." *comScore* (2007): http://www.comscore.com/Press_Events/Press_Releases/2007/10/Worldwide_Searches_Reach_61_Billion.

Longenecker, Clinton O., and Laurence S. Fink, "Management training: Benefits and lost opportunities (part II)." *Industrial and Commercial Training* 37, no 2. (2005): 73-79.

Madden, Mary. "The audience for online video-sharing sites shoots up." *Pew Internet* (2009): http://fe01.pewinternet.org/Reports/2009/13--The-Audience-for-Online-VideoSharing-Sites-Shoots-Up.aspx.

Martin, Lilian Hayes. *The business devotional.* Sterling Innovation 2009.

Mercer. "Human capital planning 2010: Resetting the talent and rewards agenda." (2009): http://www.mercer.com/attachment.

dyn?idContent=1356290&filePath=/attachments/English/
HCP2010_POV_final.pdf.

Morales, Lymari. "Self-employed workers clock the most hours each week." *Gallup* (2009): http://www.gallup.com/poll/122510/Self-Employed-Workers-Clock-Hours-Week.aspx.

National Association of Colleges and Employers. "2009 student survey." (2009): http://www.naceweb.org/Research/Student/Student_Survey.aspx.

Neely, Robert O., and Duane Alm. "Meeting individual needs: A learning styles success story." *Clearing House* 66, no. 2 (1992): 109-113.

Neisser, Ulric. "Rising scores on intelligence tests." *American Scientist* 85, (1997): 440-447.

Nordenson, Bree. "Overload! Journalism's battle for relevance in an age of too much information." *Columbia Journalism Review* (2008): http://www.cjr.org/feature/overload_1.php.

O'Brien, Michael. "Long-distance relationship troubles." *HR Executive* (2009): http://www.hrexecutive.com/HRE/story.jsp?storyId=229836658.

Pechstein, Louis Augustus. "Massed vs. distributed effort in learning." *Journal of Educational Psychology*, 12, no. 2 (1921).

Phillips, Jack, and Patti Phillips. "The real reason we don't evaluate." *Chief Learning Officer* (2009).

Prensky, Marc. "Digital natives, digital immigrants." *On the Horizon* 9 no. 5 (2001).

Raelin, Joseph A. "Action learning and action science: Are they different?" *Organizational Dynamics*, 26 (1997): 21-34.

Rafaeli, Anat, and Robert Sutton. "Expression of emotion as part of the work role." *Academy of Management Review*, 12 (1987): 23-37.

Randstad. "Tenth annual world of work survey." (2009): http://www.us.randstad.com/.

Revans, Reginald. *Action learning: New techniques for management*. London: Blond & Briggs, Ltd., 1980.

———. *The origin and growth of action learning*. Brickley, UK: Chartwell-Bratt., 1982.

———. *ABC of action learning*. London: Lemos and Crane., 1988.

Roche, Robert. "The Wireless Association announces semi-annual wireless industry survey results." *CTIA* (2009): http://www.businesswire.com/news/google/20091007006200/en/CTIA%E2%80%93The-Wireless-Association-Announces-Semi-Annual-Wireless-Industry.

Rodgers, Eric. "Executing blended learning." *Chief Learning Officer* (2009).

Shaw, Hayden. "Modular series: Leading across generations." *Franklin Covey.*

Shipman, Claire, and Katty Kay. "Women will rule business." *Time* (2009): http://www.time.com/time/specials/packages/article/0,28804,1898024_1898023_1898078,00.html.

Sisti, Helene M., Arnold L. Glass, and Tracey J. Shors. "Neurogenesis and the spacing effect: Learning over time enhances memory and the survival of new neurons." *Learning and Memory* (2007).

Sitzmann, Traci, Kenneth Brown, Wendy Casper, Katherine Ely, and Ryan Zimmerman. "A review and meta-analysis of the nomological network of trainee reactions." *Journal of Applied Psychology* 93, no. 2 (2008): 280-295.

Sorohan, Erica Gordon. "We do; therefore we learn." *Training and Development* 4, no. 10 (1993): 47-55.

Stewart, Thomas. *The wealth of knowledge: Intellectual capital and the twenty-first century organization.* Doubleday, 2001.

Sun Microsystems. "Open work: Overview." (2009): http://www.sun.com/aboutsun/openwork/index.jsp.

Swanson, Richard A. *Assessing the financial benefits of human resource development.* Cambridge, MA: Perseus, 2001.

Thibault, Pascal, Patrick Bourgeois, and Usrula Hess. "The effect of group-identification on emotion recognition: The case of cats and basketball players." *Journal of Experimental Social Psychology,* 42 (2006): 676-683.

United States Department of Labor. "Employee tenure in 2008." *Bureau of Labor Statistics* (2008): http://www.bls.gov/news.release/tenure.htm.

―――. "Number of jobs held, labor market activity, and earnings growth among the youngest baby boomers: Results from a longitudinal survey." *Bureau of Labor Statistics* (2008): http://www.bls.gov/news.release/nlsoy.toc.htm.

―――. "Current unemployment rates for states and historical highs/lows." *Bureau of Labor Statistics* (2009): http://stats.bls.gov/web/lauhsthl.htm.

―――. "Employment projections: 2008-18." *Bureau of Labor Statistics* (2009): http://www.bls.gov/news.release/pdf/ecopro.pdf.

Van Derhei, Jack. "The impact of the recent financial crisis on

401(k) account balances." *EBRI Issue Brief,* no. 326 (2009): http://www.ebri.org/pdf/briefspdf/EBRI_IB_2-2009_Crisis-Impct.pdf.

Wakefield Research. "In-flight Wi-Fi takes off: Frequent flyers, business travelers say it tops other airline amenities." *Wi-Fi Alliance* (2009): http://www.wi-fi.org/news_articles. php?f=media_news&news_id=847.

Watson Wyatt. "WorkUSA 2006/2007: Debunking the myths of employee engagement." (2007): http://www.watsonwyatt. com/research/resrender.asp?id=2006-US-0039&page=1.

Wexley, Kenneth, and Gary Latham. *Developing and training human resources in organizations (3rd ed.),* Upper Saddle River, NJ: Prentice Hall, 2002.

www.ingramcontent.com/pod-product-compliance
Lightning Source LLC
Chambersburg PA
CBHW030005190526

45157CB00014B/428